Praise for MISSION TRIPS THAT MATTER

With uplifting anecdotes, inspiring prayers, and sound theological reflection, Don Richter offers a gift to all who desire a broad understanding of mission. His imaginative "embodied faith" approach upholds the mutuality and justice that undergird enlightened, cross-cultural efforts, rescuing mission from domination assumptions and opening the way for transformation.

—THE REVEREND JOYCE HOLLYDAY
Author and copastor of Circle of Mercy, Asheville, NC

Sometimes we are so busy *doing mission trips* that we don't take the time to *be mission*. Don Richter encourages us to see mission differently—to see mission as a pilgrimage that transcends our personal experiences and connects us with the church's mission throughout the ages, anchored in the mission of Jesus Christ. *Mission Trips That Matter* will enable you to do mission more effectively and with deeper significance. This resource will enrich ministry with our young disciples.

—BOB MCCARTY
Executive Director
National Federation for Catholic Youth Ministry

True to the method and philosophy of Christian practices published in *Practicing Our Faith* and *Way to Live*, Richter has prayerfully, liturgically, and poetically offered us a book that will no doubt be foundational for thoughtful leaders of short-term mission trips and service projects. He invites us to consider the why-tos and imagine new how-tos as we engage youth and adults in the formative journey of mission work.

—EVELYN L. PARKER
Associate Professor of Christian Education
Perkins School of Theology
Southern Methodist University

Mission trips can be great experiences of learning, growth, and service. But they can also be a waste of time or worse. What makes the difference? Don Richter has explored the elements of successful mission trips and offers his insights in this very readable book. *Mission Trips That Matter* will be an important reference for leaders of, senders for, and participants in mission trips.

—CHRISTIAN SMITH
William R. Kenan Jr. Professor of Sociology and Director
Center for the Study of Religion and Society
University of Notre Dame

Mission Trips That Matter is a timely companion for contemplation of, preparation for, and participation in missions as a practice of life-giving faith, incarnational ecclesiology, and transformational inward-outward homecoming. This book pulls into focus the why-tos of missions as experiential faith formation and prophetic action in service of God's vision of right relationship and redistributive justice—locally and globally. In an age when globalization can paralyze and intimidate us, Richter's words instruct and mobilize us for shalomalization!

—THE REVEREND KELVIN SAULS
Director of Congregational Transformation
General Board of Discipleship, United Methodist Church

Mission Trips That Matter

Embodied Faith for the Sake of the World

DON C. RICHTER

UPPER
ROOM BOOKS®
NASHVILLE

Contents

Acknowledgments

F ootnotes cite sources out of obligation, and perhaps gratitude. The acknowledgments on this page flow from a grateful heart for the personal encouragement and professional support I received while writing this book.

First and foremost I am grateful to Dorothy C. Bass, director of the Valparaiso Project on the Education and Formation of People in Faith. Since 1999 I have had the joy and privilege of serving the Valparaiso Project in various capacities, from managing grant programs and Web sites (www.practicingourfaith.org and www.wayto live.org) to coordinating the Project's work on Christian practices and youth. A highlight of this work was coediting *Way to Live* with Dorothy, one of the wisest wordsmiths and most insightful theologians I know. I am honored to be Dorothy's colleague and to have her write the foreword to *Mission Trips That Matter*.

The Valparaiso Project supported my research for writing this book. Project coordinator Doretta Kurzinski provided patient, caring assistance at every turn. Project associate Susan Briehl, a Lutheran pastor, hymn writer, and liturgist, helped seed many ideas in this book through leading a 2005 consultation on mission trips and Christian practices at Spirit in the Desert Retreat Center (Carefree, Arizona). Buoyed by Susan's artful teaching and inspired to song by Tom Witt and Mary Preus, consultation participants offered a feast of ideas based on mission experience in different settings. Special thanks to Jeremy Myers, Frank Santoni, Joyce Hollyday, Michael Cobbler, Bob Kruschwitz, Ruth Anderson, Pat Slater, Ben Johnston-Krase, Brandon Wert, Brian Cole, Carolyn Brown, Ann Laird Jones, Larry Peterson, Ron Robinson, Tina McCormick, and Rachel Tomas Morgan.

Conversations with veteran mission-trip leaders brought invaluable perspective. My deep appreciation to David Knecht, Larry Coulter, Beth Grimshaw, Trevor Hudson, Bob Chell, Marilyn Borst, Gary Hansen, Jennifer Jue, Beth McCaw, Bruce and Carolyn Gillette, Alan and Beth Claassen Thrush.

Recent mission trips helped me gain fresh perspective as I was writing. My son, Jonathan, and I participated in the mission partnership between Grace Covenant Presbyterian Church in Asheville, North Carolina, and the Jerusalem Presbyterian Church in Coatepeque, Guatemala. I accompanied Ministry of Money on a "pilgrimage of reverse mission" to Tijuana, Mexico. Group Workcamps Foundation welcomed me to observe a week of home repair and outreach in Hammond, Indiana. In 2006 the Union Church of Hinsdale, Illinois, enlisted me as an adult leader on their annual Spring Work Tour for youth. I was humbled by the heroic relief efforts on the Gulf Coast following the devastation of hurricanes Katrina and Rita. Mission teams and individuals from every quarter came to lend a hand. The only seafood I had the entire week was that first night when we dined on Alaskan salmon trucked down by a carpenter from Anchorage!

Opportunities to present ideas and refine my thinking about mission trips were made possible by the Episcopal Dioceses of North Carolina, Western North Carolina, and East Carolina; the Presbytery of Charlotte, North Carolina; Holden Village; Riverside Presbyterian Church in Jacksonville, Florida; the First United Methodist Church of Boulder, Colorado; the First Presbyterian Church of Brookings, South Dakota; the Institute for Youth Ministry at Princeton Theological Seminary (Kenda Dean, Amy Vaughn, and Dayle Gillespie Rounds); the Fund for Theological

Education (Melissa Wiginton and Kevin Spears); Austin Presbyterian Theological Seminary (Ted Wardlaw); and Garrett Evangelical Theological Seminary (Reggie Blount). Thanks to Garrett students who shared mission-trip wisdom during a January 2007 course I taught on "Growing in Faith with Youth."

I am grateful to three colleagues in ministry who reviewed early drafts of this material and offered substantive editorial comments that strengthened every chapter: Dori Baker, Susan Steinberg, and Julie Ruth Harley. My heartfelt thanks to Julie—a dear friend, confidante, and beacon of light during every phase of this writing project.

Robin Pippin and Jeannie Crawford-Lee, editors at Upper Room Books, graciously shepherded this book to publication.

Craig Dykstra, who leads the Religion Division of Lilly Endowment, Inc., has been a trusted teacher and mentor for more than twenty-five years. Craig's *Vision and Character* (1981) was a life-anchoring book for me, and set the stage for generative scholarship exploring the life of faith as informed by Christian practices. Careful readers will notice Craig's influence throughout this book.

Christian practices crystallize in worship. Central Presbyterian Church in Atlanta, Georgia, centers my worship life and my weekly coming and going. I am grateful that my daughter, Katherine, and I are nurtured by this congregation's faithfulness and strong culture of mission.

I proudly dedicate this book to Henry and Virginia Richter, my father and mother, for their abiding love and unfailing support, and for showing me what it means to follow the way of Jesus.

Don C. Richter
Decatur, Georgia
Pentecost 2007

Foreword

People of faith have been taking to the road ever since Abraham and Sarah left their home and headed into unfamiliar territory in response to God's call. They have traveled long distances to find new homes or to spread good news. They have processed as pilgrims, fled as refugees, invaded as conquerors, and gazed as tourists, exchanging both hospitality and harm with those they have met along the way. Some have undertaken outward journeys from which they never returned, while others have come safely back to the places from which their journeys began. Though their routes and outcomes have been diverse, only rarely has a traveler been unchanged, in one way or another, by the journey.

In *Mission Trips That Matter*, Don Richter considers a form of travel presently being supported by thousands of North American Christian congregations, campus ministries, and nonprofit organizations. Millions of youth and adults participate in such travel each year, crossing boundaries of neighborhood or nation to enter unfamiliar territory before returning home. Their explicit purpose is usually to serve others. Implicitly, however, sponsors also believe mission trips provide a powerful crucible for Christian formation, perhaps even for personal and social transformation. Some participants are in fact surprised by the knowledge of the world, their neighbors, themselves, and God that they gain in a short period of purposeful dislocation from familiar places and patterns of life.

In a world torn by strife and gross inequalities of wealth, safety, and opportunity, making sure mission trips matter is an urgent concern—and not only matter but matter *for the good* of both those who take the journey and those who receive them. It is no surprise that even well-intentioned trips across significant social divisions can lead to alienation rather than friendship. At the same time, isolation within enclosed communities is not a faithful option.

Don Richter is an excellent guide for those who desire to lead trips that spread hospitality rather than harm. He identifies and resists the acts that can perpetuate social and economic divisions between those who can afford to travel and the people they visit—acts that can make mission trips matter in the *wrong* way. And he shows Christian travelers how to open their eyes and hands to receive God's grace and share it with others before, during, and after such travel. Leaders who hope they and their traveling companions will be treading paths of new life for the sake of this world so loved by God will find deep wisdom and concrete help in these pages.

Don shows how mission trips hold opportunities to take up a way of life that reflects Christ's abundant life in and for the world. Exploring such a way of life is at the center of a vocation Don and I have shared for several years. With a wonderful group of teen and adult colleagues, we worked together on a book that is both precursor and companion to this one, *Way to Live: Christian Practices for Teens* (Upper Room Books, 2002). In fact, *Way to Live* begins with the story of a mission trip my daughter and I took with members of our congregation. That trip helped me to recognize the importance such journeys might hold for those who seek to embrace a way of life that reflects and responds to God's grace in Christ. When undertaken in this hope and in the power of the Holy Spirit, sharing life as servant-guests in an unfamiliar place fosters community and fresh insights into the character of life at home, even as it expands one's sense of the world beyond home.

This book's concrete focus on one setting of Christian growth is thus of a piece with the ongoing work of the Valparaiso Project to develop an understanding of Christian faith as a way of abundant life. This way of life takes shape in a set of Christian practices—things that Christian people do together over time to address fundamental human needs and conditions, in the light of and in response to God's grace to the world in Christ Jesus. (For more information on this approach and for other Project resources, please visit www.practicingourfaith.org.) Christian practices, as we understand them, bear embodied wisdom that is informed by scripture and by the experience of faithful people across centuries and cultures—wisdom about everyday living with profound implications for how we relate to God and to others in society. Those who travel together for mission and service necessarily engage in such practices: they work, rest, worship, and play; they break bread, tell stories, manage stuff, and offer welcome, friendship, and healing. Moreover, in all likelihood they do so with greater intentionality and awareness than needed at home. Mission trips thus invite Christians into conscious awareness of the practices that comprise a life-giving way of life, provide opportunities to live out those practices with others, and disclose God's presence in the midst of them through attentive prayer, conversation, and song.

As Don Richter eloquently insists, the Christian life is lived in the human body, engaging its strength and frailty and its capacities to perceive, touch, and serve. And the Christian life is lived in the Body we become as one in Christ. Thus embodied, we are instructed by scripture and surrounded by a cloud of witnesses who have been on journeys not unlike our own. Thus embodied, we are formed for life-giving journeys into the world for the sake of the world.

May the mission trips you take be journeys of just this kind. Having Don Richter as your counselor in leading a mission trip that matters will enrich your journey and the journey of those who travel with you. Godspeed in your reading, and in your travels.

Dorothy C. Bass
Valparaiso, Indiana

O God,

You have called your servants

to ventures of which

we cannot see the ending,

by paths as yet untrodden,

through perils unknown.

Give us faith to go out

with good courage,

not knowing where we go,

but only that your hand is leading us

and your love supporting us;

through Jesus Christ our Lord.

—*from* Daily Prayer *(altered)*

Introduction: Seeing Things Whole

Short-term mission trips are a booming business in this country. Each year, between two and four million North Americans load up duffel bags with clothes and supplies; stuff backpacks with hats, maps, and water bottles; and head out for a group service adventure lasting from several days to several weeks. We brave airport security lines and fly to far-flung places around the world. We board church vans and ride all night to reach distant places in the United States. We even venture into that strangest of lands called "across town."

We are people on the move. We are people on a mission.

Many of us go as members of a congregation or a youth group. A recent National Study of Youth and Religion found that 30 percent of all surveyed teenagers (ages 13–17) have gone on at least one mission trip or service project. And one out of every ten teens has gone on three or more trips. Young people value these outreach ventures as highly significant for their faith formation. Attuned to this, some youth leaders now make short-term mission trips the centerpiece of their youth ministry. How else can you corral teenagers for such a sustained block of time?

Colleges are in on the action too. Many schools offer an array of service-learning opportunities. On some campuses a spring break trip to Daytona Beach is now more alternative than repairing Katrina-ravaged houses on the Gulf Coast or playing games with children at a Costa Rican orphanage.

Eagerness to go on short-term mission trips has made such travel more than a business and more than a trend. It has become a movement. Mission trips play a significant role in the Christian formation of young people and adults. Such immersion experiences, typically outside the group's comfort zone, challenge participants to forge Christian community in ministry with others. These ventures also present an ongoing challenge to group members when they return home and attempt to understand and sustain the way of life nurtured while on the mission trip.

Seeing the Larger Story

Wise and patient leaders invite their group to look for the larger human story unfolding on a mission trip. Seeing the larger story helps mission-team members connect their travel experience to their ongoing life of faith. Instead of viewing their lives as a series of random, disconnected episodes—some good, some bad—Christians are challenged to view their own activities in relation to God's activity, their own stories in relation to God's story. Guiding folks into this way of thinking about life is at the heart of leading mission trips that matter. Consider why this is so.

On the same day, a mission-team member loses his passport; another member gets an upset stomach; and the team gathers with its host group to celebrate Communion. A trip leader may be tempted to view the Communion service as the real Christian activity while regarding the other two matters as interruptions, inconveniences that have to be managed. What if we view all three events as woven together into the very fabric of the life of faith?

Eucharist remembers profound loss and unexpected gain. At this meal, no human loss is minimized or discounted. No small talk or happy-face stickers distract participants from the pain of loss that everyone encounters in this life. A lost passport reminds us of our many losses, including the ways we can lose touch with an abiding sense of self. Identity theft, job loss, divorce, the death of a loved one—they pull the rug out from under us and send us scrambling to regain our footing.

Everyone who comes to the Table brings a legacy of loss, and we gather as a community that acknowledges these losses. Yet no one is barred from the table because of his or her losses. Paradoxically, our losses are the main course we bring to the Table and contribute to this unusual meal. Every loss is gathered up, blessed and broken, and transformed for the sake of the world. No passport? No problem! At this Table citizenship is defined by God's kingdom through the global church—not by any national boundaries. All are welcomed to this Table. The undocumented are guests of honor, for they remind the rest of us that Christ honors all equally at this feast.

Someone with an upset stomach may not feel up to joining the group for evening worship. The Eucharist invites us to pray for and tend to those who absent from the meal. We who gather re-member those not present, and the Spirit binds them to the fellowship all the same. In an age of "power lunches," this meal lifts up the powerless, the vulnerable, the ones who struggle with their bodies and their health. Jesus' own body is broken at this meal, as it was broken for disciples at the Last Supper and for the whole creation on the cross. Such a strange meal that sustains so many with so little food; that always makes room for one more guest; that never updates the menu; that sends us away hungry yet satisfied; that nourishes even those who cannot ingest the food fragments in person.

A lost passport, a sick team member, and a Communion service. Do we see three disparate, atomized events, with worship as the only definable Christian activity? Or do we see the larger story in which these three events interconnect with threads of sin and grace, fracture and healing, discouragement and hope? The more our hearts and minds are shaped by biblical and liturgical imagination, the more connections we notice as the larger story of our mission trip unfolds. And the more we notice as leaders—especially in relation to our bodies—the more readily we invite all participants to weave together daily events into the warp and woof of the life of faith.

Pondering the Body

A constant factor in every mission trip is the traveling body. Typically mission-team members travel together, so collectively we become a traveling body in that sense. A mission team also serves with neighbors to form a new community or body: a company of strangers knit together as the body of Christ.

Individual bodies travel too, so we ponder what it means for every body to be on a mission trip. Human beings are bodily creatures. We can experience the world only in and through our marvelously complex bodies—bodies that are fragile yet resilient, finite yet transcendent.

We can identify a number of ways to cultivate mindfulness about our body as we journey:

- by what we pay attention to with our eyes, listen to with our ears, notice with our nose
- by what we tote on our back and hold in our hands as we go
- by literally standing on common ground with others
- by taking in our travel experience through mouth and digestive system
- by blessing new companions with words of encouragement from our lips.

Bodies are not incidental to the mission-trip experience. They are not something we must get beyond in order to tap into the "real, spiritual aspect" of such travel. As followers of Jesus, we celebrate the mystery of Incarnation, confessing that God took on flesh to enter this world as a human being. God came to us as a sacred yet vulnerable body, a body sacred and vulnerable like our own. And when that body was crucified, God's resurrection power raised it from the dead. Just as God honored Jesus' body, so God honors all human bodies, created as we are in the very image of God.

Life in the body lies at the heart of Christian faith. We don't have religious or spiritual experiences apart from our bodies. So we need to pay careful attention to what our own body and the bodies of others are teaching us as we undertake mission trips. We need to move beyond our checklists to ponder what deeper wisdom the Spirit is whispering as we get our immunization shots, pack our bags, fill our water bottles, put on our walking shoes, strap on our cameras, and pull out our maps. It just may be that attuning ourselves to these basic, necessary travel activities can help us live more fully the loving, challenging life that Jesus himself lived and gave to his followers.

Mining the Meaning of Mission-Trip Experience

Mission Trips That Matter offers ways for leaders of short-term mission trips and service projects (sometimes called "servant trips") to mine the meaning of mission-trip experience. This approach will help groups reflect on life together as they prepare for, engage in, and return from short-term mission trips and service projects involving travel. Everyone who plans or leads such ventures for a congregation, a youth group, college students, or service agencies can use these tools, whether lay volunteers, youth leaders, outreach ministers, pastors, college chaplains, or service-learning coordinators. I hope that all mission-trip participants will find nourishment for their souls in the following pages.

Part I features two foundational chapters. "Why We Go" examines core reasons that groups go on mission trips and why this matters to the church. The mission trip is a contemporary form of pilgrimage. We'll ask how the structure of pilgrimage shapes a mission-trip experience—for better or worse. I'm not an uncritical booster for every mission trip! Leaders must separate the wheat from the chaff, providing sound theological rationale for embarking on such costly outreach efforts.

As a mission-trip leader, you have a lot weighing on your mind. And you no doubt have a lot weighing on your heart too. "Preparing to Lead" invites you to prepare your own heart as you prepare to lead others into outreach ventures. This chapter encourages you to acknowledge your personal limits, vulnerability, and control needs while accepting leadership authority and trusting in God's providence. For those who follow Jesus, leadership is grounded in the One who came among us to serve, who showed us how to gain our lives by giving them away in love.

Part II presents a series of meditations on the body. Each chapter in this section invites you to ponder your own body and the bodies of others as you are sent forth in mission. These meditations evoke the book's central message: reflect on personal mission-trip experience in light of biblical wisdom and in response to the daily manna and mercy Jesus provides. These body meditations are meant to prompt contemplation and conversation before, during, and after your trip.

Part III provides guidelines and resources for faithful travel, especially for congregations planning mission trips. "Building the Body for Mission" describes how to strengthen a culture of mission, count the cost of outreach ventures, cultivate partnerships, evaluate host agencies, simulate challenges, share your story, and bless one another for the journey. This chapter will help pastors, teachers, and mission-trip leaders make the case within their communities for sponsoring short-term mission trips. "Resources for the Road" and "Prayers for the Journey" offer additional support as you plan and lead your trip.

Each chapter in this book opens with prayer, because prayer opens you to life in the Spirit. Pray these prayers aloud, by yourself and with your group. Pray each prayer more than once, so that familiar words fall fresh on your ears. Encourage one another to learn by heart the sending prayer at the beginning of this introduction. For every journey and life transition, this "good courage" prayer grounds us in God's grace as we step out in faith. Gather up your own prayers as you go. (See also "Prayers for the Journey," page 164.) Even more than photos, prayers will chronicle your soul's pilgrimage.

Each chapter concludes with "For the Journey" learning activities and reflection questions to help your group *ponder the body* before, during, and after your trip. Engage these questions and activities with your mission team to sustain the power of your outreach venture. Instead of evaluating a mission trip as simply "an interesting experience" bracketed from daily life, infuse daily life with the practices and perspectives revealed through faithful travel. In this way, the experience continues to percolate through your hearts and minds, opening you to new insights and deeper connections to what God is calling you to be and do for the sake of the world.

Reflection doesn't happen automatically. Nor does life-centering conversation. Gather your group at regular intervals in designated places. Plan for brief gatherings while in transit—on the bus, in the van, or at an airport terminal gate. Schedule longer sessions before and after your trip and while on site with your mission partners. Choose carefully what questions you will pose and what learning activities you will lead. "For the Journey" offers a range of options, but you will need to select what best serves the needs of your group, given your mission context.

Each time you host a conversation with your group, identify your hopes for the specific people who will gather. Hoping they will grow in faith is the overarching goal, but consider proximate steps pilgrims can take along that path. For example, you may hope that mission team members will pay attention to their own hands and the hands of others throughout the day. Ask them to notice what those hands are giving and receiving; what work is being done and what care given by those hands; what signs of age and injury those hands bear. When you gather again to share hand stories, pray that God will protect and bless all those hands.

Guided by your hopes, set up a suitable space for comfortable conversation. Prepare in advance any resources and materials, improvising as necessary. Maintain an atmosphere of trust and respect as team members share, creating space for everyone's voice to be heard. Allow space for silence as well, affirming that the Spirit speaks through silence as well as through words.

Practices as Embodied Wisdom

Preparing for the journey requires reliable information, planning, resources, and coordination. Yet at every stage, good preparation also involves wisdom and discernment. The community Jesus called into being through his life and ministry is the source of this wisdom. That community continues, in the power of his Spirit, to follow Jesus' way of life today. Christian faith is not simply a set of beliefs and doctrines, important as these are. Christian faith is a way of life shaped by practices, by what Christians do in the world in response to the gift of God's grace.

Focusing on faith practices can shift mission trips from episodic, event-focused experiences to experiences woven into the larger fabric of a way of life.

Practices are embodied wisdom handed down to us by generations of faithful followers of Jesus. Wisdom about how to care for the earth and manage our stuff. Skills for making strangers feel welcome. Gestures for forgiving others, including our enemies. Even good manners for sharing food and fellowship around the dinner table and the Lord's Table. We don't just do these things with our minds; we do them with our hearts and with our hands and with our bodies. Focusing on faith practices can shift mission trips from episodic, event-focused experiences to experiences woven into the larger fabric of a way of life.

Practicing Our Faith and *Way to Live* are two vital resources to deepen your understanding of this way of life shaped by Christian practices. I highly recommend these books as background reading. See "Resources for the Road" for publication details. *Mission Trips That Matter* actually germinated from the seed of these two books. Readers asked, "How can Christian practices come into focus as a group shares life together during a mission trip?" It's fitting to see these pages as ongoing conversation sparked by the opening chapter of *Way to Live*—"Life"—which describes experiences on a youth/adult mission trip.

What You Won't Find Here

Checklists are necessary. Mission-trip leaders rely on checklists to plan activities, coordinate logistics, advise team members on how to prepare and what to pack. This book doesn't give you a laundry list of how-tos for planning and leading your trip. Instead, these chapters present the *why*-tos and suggest implications for the how-tos. Nor does this book feature a menu of fund-raising ideas, although it makes the case for supporting the cost of mission trips as a budget priority.

You won't find generic team-building games, personality inventories, and the like, useful as these are. Instead, this book focuses on building the body for mission as a matter of faith, forming ourselves as the body of Christ for the sake of the world.

As you design worship liturgy for your mission team, you'll need more actual worship resources (songs, prayers, litanies) than provided in this book. You can find additional resources at www.prac ticingourfaith.org.

This book does not attempt to offer "Everything You Need to Know about Planning and Leading a Short-Term Mission Trip." You will find crucial resources to complement this book in "Resources for the Road."

I trust that these chapters will give you vital perspectives and inspiration for making mission trips matter as you prepare to serve while you're on the road, and after you return home.

For the Journey

From October 1981 to March 1982, Dutch priest Henri Nouwen kept a journal of his mission experience in Bolivia and Peru. Read the following journal entry, penned near the end of Nouwen's six-month sojourn. What motives does Nouwen name for serving in the mission field? Which motives prompt you to serve? Nouwen claims that guilt and the desire to save can be powerful, damaging motives for serving others. Do you agree with his assessment? Why are these motives especially tempting for North Americans? How can humility and gratitude free us from guilt/savior motives as we serve others? As you read this book, look for specific ways in which your mission team can cultivate the virtues of humility and gratitude before, during, and after your trip.

Friday, March 5

The two most damaging motives in the makeup of missioners seem to be guilt and the desire to save. Both form the extremes of a long continuum, both make life in the mission extremely painful. As long as I go to a poor country because I feel guilty about my wealth, whether financial or mental, I am in for a lot of trouble. The problem with guilt is that it is not taken away by work. Hard work for the poor may push my guilt underground for a while, but can never really take it away. Guilt has roots deeper than can be reached through acts of service. On the other hand, the desire to save people from sin, from poverty, or from exploitation can be just as harmful, because the harder one tries the more one is confronted with one's own limitations. Many hard-working men and women have seen the situation getting worse during their missionary career; and if they depended solely on the success of their work, they would quickly lose their sense of self-worth. Although a sense of guilt and a desire to save can be very destructive and depressive for missioners, I do not think that we are ever totally free from either. We feel guilty and we desire to bring about change. These experiences will always play a part in our daily life.

The great challenge, however, is to live and work out of gratitude. The Lord took on our guilt and saved us. In him the Divine work has been accomplished. The human missionary task is to give visibility to the Divine work in the midst of our daily existence. When we can come to realize that our guilt has been taken away and that only God saves, then we are free to serve, then we can live truly humble lives. Clinging to guilt is resisting God's grace, wanting to be a savior, competing with God's own being. Both are forms of idolatry and make missionary work very hard and eventually impossible.

Humility is the real Christian virtue. It means staying close to the ground (*humus*), to people, to everyday life, to what is happening with all its down-to-earthness. It is the virtue that opens our eyes for the presence of God on the earth and allows us to live grateful lives. The poor themselves are the first to help us recognize true humility and gratitude. They can make a receptive missioner a truly happy person.

Part I

O God, full of compassion, we commit and commend
ourselves to you, in whom we live and move and have our being.
Be the goal of our pilgrimage, and our rest by the way.
Give us refuge from the turmoil of worldly distractions
beneath the shadow of your wings. Let our hearts, so often
a sea of restless waves, find peace in you, O God.

—*Evangelical Lutheran Worship*

1
Why We Go

Why do we go on short-term mission trips? For what purpose? Why do we invest considerable time, energy, and money in such ventures? The modern mission-trip movement is fueled by many assumptions. Here are different reasons people give for going on mission trips:

- Travel away from home takes us out of our comfort zones, challenges our sense of entitlement, and thus opens us to new experiences of ourselves and the world.
- Acquiring new habits and practices requires dehabituation, breaking our old habits and patterns. Travel effectively dehabituates, providing openings for new insights.
- Affluent North Americans need to encounter how the majority of the world's people live.
- Privileged people have a "noble obligation" (*noblesse oblige*) to serve the less fortunate.
- We learn to "count our blessings" through encounters with people less fortunate.
- "God so loved the world," so we need to get out there and love it as well.
- Jesus sends modern disciples on short-term missions, just as he sent his original followers to serve and proclaim the gospel.

As you consider the trip you're planning or have taken, with which of the statements above would you agree? Which strike you as most compelling? Which do you find problematic and why? Add your own guiding assumptions to this list. Then see which assumptions you detect in the following "parable" currently circulating throughout cyberspace:

> One day the father of a wealthy suburban family takes his son on a trip to the country to show the lad how poor people live. They spend a couple of days and nights on the farm of what would be considered a poor family.
>
> On their return trip, the father asks his son, "Well, what did you think?"
>
> "It was great, Dad."
>
> "Did you see how poor people live?" the father asks.
>
> "Oh yeah," says the son.
>
> "So, tell me, what did you learn from our trip?" asks the father.
>
> The son replies: "I learned that we have one dog, and they have four. We have a pool that reaches to the middle of our garden, and they have a creek that has no end. We have imported lanterns in our garden, and they have the stars at night. Our patio reaches to the front yard, and they have the whole horizon. We have a small piece of land to live on, and they have fields that go beyond our sight. We have servants who serve us, but they serve others. We buy our food, but they grow theirs. We have walls around our property to protect us; they have friends to protect them."
>
> The boy's father is speechless.
>
> Then his son adds, "Thanks, Dad, for showing me how poor we are."

Wising Up

This fictional story doesn't describe a mission trip per se. Even so, it's a parable for those of us who go on such trips. A parable holds up a mirror and invites us to gaze into it through the eyes of our own experience. What do we see when we gaze into this mirror?

First, let's consider why the father takes his son on this trip. Is he motivated by compassion or a desire to serve others? Hard to judge someone's motives, though the story says the father hopes to teach his son a lesson by dramatizing the difference between rich and poor people. The parable's premise is not outrageous; people do sometimes travel for such purposes.

In some affluent congregations, parents support youth mission trips with the explicit hope that their children will learn to count their blessings. "My kids take so much for granted," exclaimed one mother. "I want them to get a clue about how good they have it in our country, living with our family." We may not say it so directly, but is this one of our tacit hopes for participants when leading a mission trip? Is it wrong to hope for such awareness?

Notice in the story how the son's view of wealth subverts the father's view. When it comes to what really matters in life, the boy concludes, the poor farm family is truly rich, while he and his dad are the poor ones. We often hear similar testimonies from returning mission teams. Perhaps you yourself have been humbled by the resourcefulness, dignity, and joy you've encountered in the Two-Thirds World.

One can admire the assets and faithfulness of impoverished communities without romanticizing poverty, however. One can extol the virtues of poor people while also confronting unjust conditions—including our own lifestyle choices—that make and keep them poor.

A parable is a sounding board as well as a mirror. When you listen to this story, where do you hear the voices of "the poor family"? Perhaps you don't hear their voices because in this story their voices don't count. They are truly the ones left "speechless," it seems. Granted, the story provides glimpses of their agency—they care for animals, grow their own food, practice mutual aid—but mostly they function as ciphers or place-holders in the story. We never hear what the farm family thinks about the rich folks' escapade. Did the farm family have any life-centering conversations with the boy or his father? Did they get a chance to share their joys and sorrows? We don't know and can only imagine.

In fact, this story doesn't even invite us to imagine a conversation with the farm family, because in the end, it's not about them at all. It's about the agenda of the wealthy father and son. And it's about the father accomplishing his goal of enlightening the son, though in a different direction than anticipated. The son thanks his father for this lesson, but there's no guarantee that wising up leads to a better way of life for anyone.

Christian faith wises us up in a different way. Christian faith gives us gospel wisdom for venturing forth into the world. In Jesus, this kind of wisdom ventured forth as a human being, gathered and taught disciples not in a school building but while on the road. Jesus sent his followers as apostles ("sent ones") into every corner of the world. Indeed, those early Christians were known simply as "people of the way." They didn't travel out of mere curiosity or wanderlust. They didn't go to browbeat folks with their Bibles either—the New Testament had yet to be written. Jesus' followers venture forth into the world to share a way of life with others, a gospel-shaped life so dynamic that it continuously spills across all cultural boundaries and humanly defined borders.

Creation on the Move

Both upper arms are sore from the shots I got this morning at the DeKalb County Health Department. With my trip to Mexico only weeks away, I needed a ten-year booster for tetanus and diphtheria and a second dose of the hepatitis A vaccine (the first dose was for a mission trip four years ago). I also got an antibiotic to take along in the event I'm stricken with the Tijuana trots.

I feel reluctant going to the medical clinic any time but especially in midwinter when waiting rooms are filled with sick folk. To heighten my anxiety, one of the physician assistants wears a face mask to prevent broadcasting her germs as she coughs vigorously.

How ironic—to protect my health I make a pilgrimage to Contagion Central!

Brett Webb-Mitchell wisely observes that "the education of a pilgrim begins with the simplest movement of the foot forward." We learn most profoundly by doing, by physically setting forth on the journey. Yet that first step on the journey begins long before the actual trip. My Tijuana journey began months ago, as I read books and articles about border issues. I wrote an autobiographical statement to share with travel companions from around the country. Numerous e-mail exchanges have kept the trip on my mind long before I grab my bags and head for the airport.

Getting vaccinated is one more prompt for reflection. I'm getting those shots to inoculate me against harmful microbes I'll probably encounter while on the road. Traveling to an unfamiliar place puts my body at risk; insofar as I'm able, I'll try to preserve my health and prevent myself from getting sick. My travel companions are required to get shots as well. We don't want to burden one another by becoming ill in a foreign land.

Human beings are not the only ones on the move though. What about the germs I'll carry down to Mexico? How will I be putting the people there at risk by transporting harmful microbes on my body? Microbes for which their bodies are unprepared? One tragic strand of colonial history in the Americas is the decimation of native populations by smallpox and other European-borne plagues. Disease caused more deaths than weapons.

Germs are clever. They find ingenious ways to travel long distances by co-opting the mobile animal kingdom. So do plants. Throughout the Southeastern U.S., the imported Japanese vine kudzu was planted for erosion control until folks realized it was colonizing the entire landscape. Flourishing in this ideal climate, kudzu grows as much as a foot per day, climbing trees, telephone poles, houses, and every vertical object it touches. Leave your window open at night, and kudzu will join you at the breakfast table in the morning.

For better or worse, invasive, nonnative species are everywhere. They generally settle in, adapt, and sometimes thrive in their adopted niche due to lack of predators. People migrate to live in different places too. We also travel for other reasons and with the goal of returning home. Pilgrimage is a common, traditional form of destination travel.

Pilgrimage through the Centuries

A pilgrimage sets things in motion, creates a new field of relationships, and often produces unintended consequences. A pilgrim has a destination, yet realizes that the most significant life lessons about oneself, others, and God may be learned along the way toward that destination. Freed Hebrew slaves encountered God during forty years of wandering in the wilderness, on their circuitous path toward the Promised Land. So formative was this period that the people later portrayed their covenantal identity and laws in light of what was revealed to them in the desert. The faith that became Judaism was forged by a people in exile, struggling to "sing the Lord's song in a foreign land."

Since the fourth century Christians have made pilgrimage to Jerusalem, though not without ambivalence about the enterprise. Even advocates such as Saint Jerome emphasized growth in faith over devotion to holy sites and relics. "Happy are those who carry Bethlehem in their own hearts, in whose hearts Christ is born every day," Jerome said. The practice of pilgrimage has persisted throughout church history, however. The physical journey of pilgrimage is a compelling metaphor for the life of faith. Why is this so?

A pilgrimage, like the life of faith, involves transformation. The pilgrim first separates from the known world. Donning distinctive clothing and carrying special provisions, the pilgrim enters *liminal*, or threshold, space while on the road. Think of this as "bewixt-and-between space," such as the space where a bride and groom find themselves during a wedding ceremony. Life-defining change often occurs during this liminal phase, when the pilgrim is literally in transition and reality seems in flux. The pilgrim finally returns home and is reincorporated, just as a married couple is introduced to guests as a new entity after the ceremony. The rite of passage is complete.

In medieval Europe, pilgrimage provided temporary liberation from tightly controlled, hierarchical feudal society. Pilgrims traveled outward and away from home toward a shrine or sacred place, and left behind the constraints and concerns of their designated life stations. Social scripts were suspended as pilgrims hit the road and entered liminal space where roles were fluid and where they could reinvent themselves and write their own life stories. More importantly, pilgrims played their part in the larger life drama of salvation, accompanied by that most trustworthy cast of characters, the communion of saints.

In medieval Europe, pilgrimage provided temporary liberation from tightly controlled, hierarchical feudal society.

✦

Communitas describes the liminal social space created when people are temporally bound together by their common humanity rather than by their social status. Ordinarily a prince and pauper would rarely converse and never mix as equals. On pilgrimage, they might chat for hours and even share a meal together over a campfire. When they return home, though, the party's over as social roles are reinstated. In this regard, classical pilgrimage critiqued but maintained the status quo. Pilgrims may have returned home transformed in spirit. Yet they were expected to pick up where they left off, resuming the roles and responsibilities of their designated life stations.

The Protestant Reformation renounced and even banned pilgrimage as a devotional practice, claiming it smacked too much of works-righteousness. In place of the physical journey toward holiness, Protestants emphasized the interior faith journey of every Christian and pilgrimage as allegory (think *Pilgrim's Progress*). Instead of leaving kin behind to join the company of saints somewhere out there, the Protestant path from Luther on has elevated the calling of every disciple to tend hearth and nurture family. During the centuries since the Reformation, Roman Catholics sustained the practice of pilgrimage-as-journey for the Western church.

Inverting or Preserving the Status Quo?

In our time the mission trip has emerged as a contemporary form of pilgrimage among Christians of every stripe. Mission trips draw on the structure of classical pilgrimage: traveling away from home, shared liminality and practices on the road, Communion with "saints" in distant lands, and returning with a transformed heart. Mission-trip veterans yearn for the life-centering community they've encountered while on the road.

If the mission trip is a modern-day pilgrimage, what is the social world such a trip inverts? What social world does it preserve? Could it be that mission trips gain their power by temporarily inverting our everyday worlds, only to reimmerse us in these worlds without challenging the way we live? Do we go on these trips to experience a *communitas* high, only to return with no strategy for ongoing transformation?

This is certainly a danger, given our consumer-driven culture. I can consume mission-trip experiences the same way a typical tourist consumes excursions. I can "go native" for awhile, knowing all the time I'll return to my comfortable routines and privileges and continue life as before. This approach reinforces confidence in consumer culture and makes me feel "blessed" to be a beneficiary of the status quo. As travel counselor Rick Steves laments,

> American Christians care about people; we've got good hearts. . . . I get so frustrated when a church group goes down to Tijuana, builds a house, and comes back and does not incorporate that compassion in an enlightened kind of citizenship. I want them to be active Christian citizens, mobilized to make our country a positive force on this

planet when it comes to peace and justice issues. It's too convenient to go down to Tijuana, build a house, come back, and then vote for your own self-interest.

Consumer culture is a powerful force that colonizes every corner of the earth. A mission trip can awaken consciousness of this force as participants catch themselves interpreting their experience using consumer categories: "How do folks have any fun without television?" or "I could really go for a Big Mac right now." These are not trivial observations. They are significant comments, for they give voice to a worldview suffused by consumer values. Such comments open the door to deeper reflection about our reliance on consumer culture. Together, we can then explore faithful, life-enhancing strategies for resistance.

In *Branded: Adolescents Converting from Consumer Faith*, Katherine Turpin claims that "mission trips embody a lived theology that directly counters consumer tenets." Turpin notes how service freely given contradicts the consumer precept of assured return for investment. Service that promotes social responsibility subverts consumer faith that prizes personal satisfaction and enrichment. Practices of compassion call participants to solidarity with those who find themselves on the underside of consumer culture.

Mission trips *implicitly* present an alternative way of life that challenges consumer culture. This subtle curriculum will fly under the radar, however, unless leaders call attention to what is life-draining and to what is life-giving during a mission trip. An alternative way of life can continue to take root as we become more intentional about life-giving practices when we return home and abide in Christian community (*koinonia*).

Communitas is fleeting, confined as it is to particular space and time. Christian community is enduring, embodied in particular times and places while also transcending time and space. Christian community comes to us as a gift of the Spirit. It's not something we can manufacture or will to happen. *Koinonia* can and does occur in conjunction with mission-trip *communitas*. It does not evaporate, however, when the effervescence of *communitas* fades.

"You Can't Go Home Again"

Pilgrimage privileges the personal mountaintop experience. Mission trips favor the team experience, though the personal dimension is always emphasized too. Trips are often billed as "life-changing" for participants. When someone does return home all fired up, who will confirm the change and help the person sustain their newfound passions? Likewise, what about folks who return home disappointed, even embarrassed, because they didn't experience the same spiritual high as others? How can leaders support both groups of people?

Thomas Wolfe was right in saying "you can't go home again." When you're away from home for any length of time, whether you have a life-altering experience or not, your sense of "home" changes because you have changed. And the folks back home aren't standing still—they're changing as well. So the homecoming experience always presents a challenge, as persons returning home seek to be accepted and reintegrated.

Mission-trip leaders can help participants return home and sustain their outreach experience by focusing on Christian practices. For all team members, leaders can call attention to ways in which particular practices have been strengthened throughout the course of the trip. And we can invite team members to continue growing in these same practices as they reenter their home context.

For instance, if mission-team members wise up regarding the grip of consumer culture in their lives, give them resources such as the "Stuff" chapter in *Way to Live* to deepen their understanding of Christian stewardship. Also strategize how to hold one another accountable for consumer habits. Take a personal clutter inventory, listing items you don't really need or use but can't bear to part with. Share this inventory with accountability partners, suggesting ways to divest unnecessary belongings.

Mutual accountability is crucial to sustaining changed behavior. We all need companions to keep us on faithful paths of discipleship, to say yes to what is life-giving and no to what is life-draining. We recognize our need for companions while on the road but need their support just as much after returning home. Homecoming can mean a head-on collision with competing loyalties. We'll turn our attention to this challenge in the next chapter.

For the Journey

Have you ever been on a trip you would consider a pilgrimage? What was your destination? With whom did you travel? What memories of hospitality—given and received—are connected to this trip? Who or what helped you integrate your travel experience when you returned home?

Identify ways in which a mission trip is like and unlike a pilgrimage. How might using the term *pilgrimage* reframe the way your mission team prepares for its service venture?

What hopes or expectations do you hold for mission-trip participants? As they go forth to serve, to what will they be asked to say yes? To what will they need to say no?

As you prepare for your trip, what is the greatest concern you have about your body? While on the road, what is the biggest challenge you face regarding your body?

Invite your leadership team to read *Honoring the Body*, by Stephanie Paulsell. Paulsell describes many of the same focal practices—bathing, eating, resting, exerting—that are central to this book. A study guide for *Honoring the Body* is available in the online library of www.practicingourfaith.org.

This chapter makes the claim that "Christian community comes to us as a gift of the Spirit. It's not something we can manufacture or will to happen." Recall a time when you experienced Christian community as an unexpected gift. How has this experience inspired you to seek such community (*koinonia*) in other places?

Watch the video in which travel counselor Rick Steves explains his convictions about "faithful travel" (see "Resources for the Road"). With what positions do you agree and disagree? How does Steves challenge people of faith to consider ourselves ambassadors of peace and justice as we travel throughout the world?

The contrast between pilgrim and tourist is often portrayed as follows: the pilgrim climbs and descends the mountain on foot; the tourist rides up the mountain via cable car, snaps a few pictures and buys souvenirs, then rides the cable car back down. Do you think this is a fair portrayal? Consider ways tourism might be undertaken with a pilgrim spirit. For example, my Aunt Evelyn has been an avid tourist during her senior years of life. While in China, she befriended persons and sponsored them to study in the United States. Ecotourism is an emergent form of tourism that promotes environmental integrity and sustainability. Think of other examples in which tourists can be ambassadors for goodwill.

I arise today

Through a mighty strength:

God's power to guide me,

God's might to uphold me,

God's eyes to watch over me;

God's ear to hear me,

God's word to give me speech,

God's hand to guard me,

God's way to lie before me,

God's shield to shelter me,

God's host to secure me.

—Saint Patrick

2
Preparing to Lead

One Sunday morning, as my pastor was praying for peace in war-ravaged Iraq, she blurted out, "Break our hearts, O God, by those very things that break your heart every day." Throughout the congregation, I could hear quiet sighs and even a few muffled "Yes, Lord's"—which is about as close as we Presbyterians allow ourselves to get to shouting "Amen!" Our pastor's prayer had struck a deep chord; her words welcomed a truth deeper than we dared utter ourselves.

"Break our hearts, O God . . ."

Why would anyone ask God for a broken heart? Don't we usually implore God to mend our broken hearts? Who in her right mind prays for more pain and suffering? Doesn't daily life serve up enough trouble and woe?

Most of us have problems aplenty that annoy and inconvenience us. When we turn on our computer and we're besieged by all manner of threats: spyware, adware, viruses, and unbidden pop-ups. And that's just in the virtual world! In the material world, we're nagged by health problems, debts, strained relationships. We also worry about the physical safety and well-being of those we love.

These are all legitimate concerns. It's important to care about family and friends, the circle of companions with whom we share life. Yet

Jesus calls us to enlarge our circle of companions, to expand compassion beyond the boundaries of our present awareness. Jesus ate meals with misfits and outcasts as well as with his friends. Jesus healed the daughter of a Gentile woman, even as he claimed that his main mission was to save the Jews. When I imagine Jesus staring into that woman's insistent face, I believe his own heart was broken and his compassion enlarged by God's boundless mercy. All of us, it seems, are candidates to be stretched Godward by compassion coaching.

Ventures of Compassion

Leading a mission trip requires many things. Most importantly, leaders are charged to guide others on a venture of compassion. Leaders accompany people into places where they may be moved by what they experience in serving others and standing in solidarity with them. South African pastor Trevor Hudson identifies compassionate caring as the distinguishing mark of faithful discipleship: "Compassionate caring creatively balances the inward-outward dynamic so characteristic of Jesus' life, saves us from falling prey to the latest fad in the spiritual supermarket, and catapults our lives into a deeper engagement with the brokenness of our world." Hudson goes on to claim that making a pilgrimage with those who suffer is one practical way to cultivate the "grace-soaked gift" of compassion in our lives.

Leaders accompany people into places where they may be moved by what they experience in serving others and standing in solidarity with them.

It's risky business, however, leading people to care for others beyond their tribe. Recall from the previous chapter how anxious we're rendered by suspicion of scarcity: "If care is in limited supply, shouldn't I give first dibs to my family and friends? Giving attention to others will distract me from caring for my primary wards. Besides, trying to address the needs of people I don't know seems presumptuous and patronizing. There's plenty of caring needed right here, among people I already know."

People may not say these things directly to leaders. Yet leaders need to anticipate that some people may feel a creeping sense of disloyalty when their companions make a pilgrimage of compassion. Leaders are the ones in charge, after all, the ones to blame for leading mission-team members astray, causing them to be preoccupied by that homeless family in Appalachia or that Mexican orphan or that village in Kenya that needs clean water. Leaders are the ones inciting well-meaning people to forsake their own tribe for the sake of serving people elsewhere.

Cultivating compassion can be costly.

Jesus got into a heap of trouble on this front. The big law firms of his day—the scribes and Pharisees—despised Jesus for eating with "unclean people." The religious and medical establishment—headed by priests—accused Jesus of malpractice: healing the wrong folks on the wrong day and in the wrong way. These Jewish authorities conspired with the Roman occupation force to condemn and execute Jesus for what they took to be disloyalty to his own people.

Cultivating compassion can be costly. Just ask Will Campbell, a Baptist minister who got the cold shoulder from fellow civil rights workers when he befriended a member of the Ku Klux Klan. "Traitor to the cause!" they muttered with disdain. Or ask the college student branded "unpatriotic" for attending the annual Vigil to Close the School of the Americas (SOA; now WHINSEC, the Western Hemisphere Institute for Security Cooperation). She spent a semester in Central America, where she met survivors of atrocities committed by SOA-trained militia. Back in the U.S.A. she travels each November across the country to join thousands who gather outside the gates of Fort Benning (Georgia) to pray and protest. Even her own family members don't understand why she gets so impassioned about this cause.

Cruciform Loyalty

Our primary loyalty to Jesus does not obliterate our loyalty to family and friends. Indeed, as Jesus' disciples we are called to faithful service with particular people in whatever particular place we find ourselves.

All human loyalties are reordered by the way of the cross, however. Loyalty that is cross-shaped calls us to love our enemies instead of harming them. Cruciform loyalty calls us to stand in solidarity with people throughout the world, regardless of national boundaries or corporate interests. Cruciform loyalty calls us to acts of risky compassion, for which we may be branded as "traitors," in league with folks like Will Campbell and that SOA protester.

Mission-trip leaders need to prepare their hearts for the competing loyalties inevitable when reaching out to others. On the one hand, leaders are responsible for the health and safety of their mission-team members and must honor legitimate family requests to "bring 'em back alive." A mission trip always involves some degree of risk taking. As the trip unfolds, leaders must continually assess whether the risk entailed is acceptable or dictates curtailing an activity.

As the trip unfolds, leaders must continually assess whether the risk entailed is acceptable or dictates curtailing an activity.

On the other hand, a mission trip may draw us into God's ways that challenge comfortable, familiar ways. In *Leadership on the Line*, Ron Heifetz and Marty Linsky observe that "when leadership counts, when you lead people through difficult change, you challenge what people hold dear—their daily habits, tools, loyalties, and ways of thinking—with nothing more to offer perhaps than a possibility." The experience of disloyalty to our deep attachments is painful, Heifetz and Linsky note: "Refashioning loyalties is some of the toughest work in life." This is especially tough work when it involves deeply held loyalties that bind us to people whom we love, especially to our own flesh and blood.

My now retired dad worked his whole career in the personnel department ("human resources") of a major chemical company. Today this company markets genetically-modified plants such as corn throughout the global south. These plants threaten biodiversity and breed dependency among farmers, who must annually purchase a fresh supply of company-produced seed and pesticide. Friends in Guatemala will suffer the long-term consequences of such unsustainable agriculture. So I feel called to speak out against this corporation's business practices, even though it feels like a betrayal, as though I'm "biting the hand that feeds me." I'm caught between competing loyalties: grateful to the company for my dad's many years of steady employment yet critical of their present actions.

Worship provides the sure way to center ourselves in the midst of these clashing allegiances. The waters of baptism remind us of our primary identity as Jesus' beloved disciples. The word proclaimed reminds us that our stories are graciously linked to God's unfolding story of salvation. And the bread and cup remind us that Jesus betrays betrayal, taking every disloyalty upon himself to be nailed to the cross with him once and for all. As leaders we serve under his mercy and with confidence that we need not shoulder the burden of reconciling everybody's competing loyalties. Jesus has already accomplished this for us. Through him, the Spirit labors to reconcile all things to God. (See Eph. 2:11-22; Col. 1:15-23.) We are at best midwives.

Leadership Team

Effective leadership is a group effort. For contact purposes and signatures, one person may need to be designated "group leader." Yet whenever possible, find ways to act in concert as a *leadership team*. Working together, you can draw on collective wisdom, balance personalities, strengthen leadership authority, and prevent individuals from becoming "the heavy" in discipline cases. Resist the temptation to call the shots yourself simply because it seems more expedient.

Leaders bear responsibility for shaping community whenever *communal care and discipline* are being exercised. Instead of viewing rule violations as challenges to authority, consider ways in which a violation presents a teachable moment, an opportunity for the community to define its norms, expectations, and boundaries. Convene an ad hoc governance council comprised of representatives from your whole mission team. Think together in advance about how this council will function in hearing and deliberating disciplinary cases that may arise.

A mission trip presents many *technical challenges* that can be addressed by available know-how. When someone loses a passport, one of the team leaders can assist in contacting the embassy for a replacement. But during a trip, a group also encounters various *adaptive challenges* for which a solution may not be obvious. A flood causes mud slides that block the road to your next destination. Your scheduled activities must be postponed or cancelled. How will your group adapt to this new situation? Who will make the necessary decisions about how to proceed?

Participants instinctively look to team leaders to "fix the problem," yet this strategy may not lead to the most creative and faithful path to follow. If leaders understand the situation as an adaptive challenge, they can give the work back to the group, designing a process to engage group members in discerning a way forward. The group may resist this work and shove it back toward the leaders. "Generally," as Heifetz and Linsky note, "people will not authorize someone to make them face what they do not want to face." Yet wise and patient leaders persist, enlisting the group to own the problem and thereby to own the solution.

A Story of Adaptive Challenge

During the summer of 1994 I was leading a theology academy for youth and adults at Emory University in Atlanta. We had planned a service day for our group with Habitat for Humanity in Americus, Georgia, where this ministry was founded. Heavy rains caused extensive flooding throughout Georgia, however. The university campus sustained minor water damage, but communities such as Americus were devastated by overflowing rivers. The roads into Americus remained impassable on the day of our scheduled trip.

Our leadership team managed the campus situation as a technical challenge, securing new meeting space for classes with waterlogged rooms. We could have treated the Americus trip as a technical challenge too, by making an executive decision that our group would simply spend a day working at the Atlanta Food Bank. That would have been worthy service and a logistical piece of cake. Instead, we considered the flooding as an adaptive challenge that called for imaginative, faithful response by a community of scholars dedicated to serving the public good.

As leaders, we first gathered the whole group and explained the situation as best we understood it. We showed video clips and read newspaper articles about the flooding. We reminded ourselves of our calling to be public theologians, to serve God through serving the common good. Then we conducted a focused innovation process that included Bible study, contemplative prayer, brainstorming, and improvisation games. Play is not frivolous activity but frees the heart and mind to entertain new possibilities. Play was crucial to our discernment process.

After four hours of discernment, of sifting through various courses of action, our group identified and carried out three related strategies in response to the flood:

(a) We volunteered with relief agencies such as the Red Cross that were already providing assistance.

(b) We organized a later trip to Americus and worked with Habitat for Humanity to lay sod on flooded property.

(c) We planned and conducted a public worship service for flood victims called "Soaking Up the Waters," grounded in the Genesis flood story in which "God remembered Noah and all the wild animals and all the domestic animals that were with him in the ark" (Gen. 8:1).

Through these efforts, youth and adults responded to an adaptive challenge by becoming a community of moral courage and care for the sake of others, for the sake of the world.

Staying Afloat

Just as staying afloat depends on team effort, staying afloat also requires an honest reckoning of personal limits, compensating as necessary for the points where a leader feels challenged. If one person is not good at details, fine—just make sure someone else has that skill. If one team member has high control needs, pair that person with someone who's comfortable going with the flow. Build a team of colleagues who will hold one another accountable for getting enough rest, eating healthy foods, and taking care of their hearts physically as well as spiritually.

Stay afloat on the waters of baptism. This is how we tend the leader's heart.

Sometimes leaders will be held accountable by those whom we least expect. In *Making Spiritual Sense*, Scott Cormode tells of a pastor who leads mission-trip participants through renewal of baptism vows as they prepare to leave. She has them take their vows again and anoints them with water from a bowl. This sending ritual casts the mission team's activity on a grander stage, reminding youth and adults that they are being sent as agents of reconciliation and ambassadors for Christ. The ritual recasts the church as a sending church like the early church at Antioch, where followers of Jesus were first known as "Christians" (Acts 11:26).

Following one particular trip, this pastor and her husband had an argument over dinner. Their spat affected the mood of the whole family. Later that evening, their four-year-old son found his mom in the basement silently folding laundry. He walked up to her with a bowl of water and proclaimed, "Mommy, I think you and Daddy need to renew your baptism."

Stay afloat on the waters of baptism. This is how we tend the leader's heart.

And this is how we care for the mission team as a body, a body that is in faith-centered motion, on pilgrimage.

For the Journey

As leaders, reflect on what gifts each member of your mission team might contribute to your trip. In what ways can you, as leaders, draw out these gifts and weave them into the life you will share together while on the road? (It helps to have a photo of each team member to contemplate.)

When have you experienced a poorly governed community? What changes in ordering, caring, and leadership were called for? When have you experienced healthy community? In what ways did this community create a space for your gifts and talents?

When was the last time your heart was broken by the situations that break God's heart? What words or images moved you, and what emotions were provoked? How does this sense of compassion shape your capacity to lead others?

Talk with church/community leaders at your host site. Ask them to name three challenges their community currently faces. Now share three challenges your own community is facing. Identify similarities and differences.

In Luke 14:26 Jesus warns his followers, "Whoever comes to me and does not hate father and mother, wife and children, brothers and sisters, yes, and even life itself, cannot be my disciple." Why would Jesus ask us to hate our closest circle of relationships for his sake? Stanley Hauerwas maintains that Jesus' scandalous saying forces disciples to reckon with what we're prepared to do to protect our dearest loves. We regularly sanction violence to defend the possessions and people we cherish. We may even take up the sword ourselves out of loyalty to family, friends, and country, or "to preserve freedom and democracy"—though the more abstract, the more difficult it is to muster that fighting spirit. An army of relative strangers is organized into platoons so that troops will fight to protect their buddies, not grand political ideas. The key to nonviolence, claims Hauerwas, is to subject all tribal loyalties to Jesus, the Prince of Peace, who commands us to love our enemies. How does this interpretation of Luke 14:26 illumine the nature of cruciform loyalty? In what areas has Christian faith produced competing loyalties for you? How do you mediate these competing loyalties?

Read about the practice of "Shaping Communities" in *Practicing Our Faith*. In every human community, leaders are stewards of this practice as they choreograph three activities: gathering the folks, breaking the bread, and telling the stories. Consider how these three basic activities shape your own faith community. Who summons people to gather? What form does that gathering take? Who is welcome to the assembly and to the Table, and who is not? Who breaks and distributes the bread—not just the Eucharist but all vital resources? Who is authorized to tell the community-defining stories? Is space provided for people to tell alternative or dissenting stories? How will your prior experience in shaping community inform the way you lead a mission trip?

Part II

You mark us with your water,

You scar us with your name,

You brand us with your vision,

> *and we ponder our baptism, your water,*
>
> > *your name,*
> >
> > *your vision.*

While we ponder, we are otherwise branded.

> *Our imagination is consumed by other brands,*
>
> > *—winning with Nike,*
> >
> > *—pausing with Coca-Cola,*
> >
> > *—knowing and controlling with Microsoft.*

Re-brand us,

> *transform our minds,*
>
> > *renew our imagination.*
> >
> > *that we may be more fully who we are marked*
> >
> > *and hoped to be,*
> >
> > *we pray with candor and courage. Amen.*

—Walter Brueggemann

3
Attentive Eyes

North American travelers often view the world through the lens of a camera. With many new sights clamoring to be seen, a camera focuses attention by bringing specific objects into view. A camera literally frames a travel experience: it frames what we see while on the road, and it frames the travel stories we tell after returning home. A camera can also provide snapshots of how we view the world prior to our journey.

Before setting forth on a summer mission trip, youth from University Presbyterian Church (Austin, Texas) used disposable cameras to take pictures of "home" to show their young mission partners in Reynosa, Mexico. The Mexican youth received cameras and the same instructions. When youth compared their photos of home, the Texans noticed that most of their photos depicted possessions, while most Mexicans took pictures of people. What both groups saw with their cameras reflects their different views of the world. The Texan team wondered long and hard about why their worldview seems more defined by stuff than by relationships. They pondered how to pay more attention to family and friends.

Cameras can enlarge or restrict our view of reality. The camera viewfinder frames selected images that confirm and reinforce our worldview. Even without the aid of a camera, we all see the world through our own personal "viewfinder," our own way of organizing reality. No one has a detached, objective view of reality guided solely by intellect and reason. We all see and interpret the world through a cultural lens that may as readily be nearsighted as clear-sighted.

Mapping the World We See

Maps, like cameras, can also enlarge or restrict our view of reality. Maps provide a schematic representation of the world. More than this, maps portray assumptions about a field of relationships. Look at a current map of North America. In the mid-seventeenth century, nautical maps extrapolated the Baja peninsula and depicted the entire state of California as an island. Spanish explorers even carried flatboats across the Sierra Nevada Mountains, reckoning they would reach the Strait of California that would take them all the way to Puget Sound. Imagine their surprise when they discovered a vast desert instead of seashore on the other side of those mountains!

Word got back that California was mainland and not an island, but for decades cartographers continued publishing the erroneous map. When corrected maps finally became available, they were not declared official for another hundred years. The authorities preferred those familiar, faulty maps that confirmed how they wished to view the world. They clung to their perception, even in the face of eye-witness testimony.

Modern maps show California as one of the forty-eight contiguous states within the United States. Adjoining California, the Baja peninsula is now mapped as Mexican territory. For millennia, people and wildlife scurried back and forth across this borderland at will, unconcerned about lines on maps. Today a tall fence slices through this borderland, built on the border, a line of black ink on paper maps.

Large metal sheets harvested from aircraft landing strips during the first Persian Gulf War form the fence. Some folks look at this rusty, corrugated border fence and see "homeland security." Residents of Tijuana look at the same fence and see a "Wall of

Shame." Along the Mexican side of the fence, shrines commemorate men, women, and children who have died while trying to cross the border. Ecologists view this long, impassible fence as a barrier disrupting the migratory patterns of flora and fauna.

How can people look at that same border fence and see it so differently?

Communities of Vision

Our way of seeing the world—for better or for worse—is profoundly shaped by various communities of vision. A political leader views the border fence from the vantage point of political and economic communities. These communities promote a worldview based on constitutional law, commerce, maps, and passports. An ecologist belongs to a community that views the world from the perspective of natural systems and processes. The ecologist doesn't ignore political realities but is compelled to observe how the border fence impacts the immediate environment. Communities of vision teach us what to pay attention to and how to describe what we notice.

A mission team can become a community of vision for team members. As discussed in the introduction, wise leaders invite participants to see the larger story unfolding on their mission trip. Often this means noticing what's right before their eyes, seeing and then seeing again, looking beyond surface appearances. Often this means seeing a web of relationships that doesn't seem obvious or apparent. For Christians, seeing the larger story always means viewing their mission-trip activities in relation to God's activity, as woven together into the fabric of the life of faith.

Prayer is what enables a mission team to become a life-centering community of vision for mission team members. Prayer involves words and conversation, to be sure. Yet prayer is first and foremost a way of seeing the world with attentive eyes. We learn to pray about what we notice, as God gives us eyes of faith and a community in which to share our vision. Prayer opens our eyes to see the contours of God's grandeur and grace in this world. Prayer also prods us to pay attention to the broken and sin-scarred places we would rather not notice.

Not long ago I participated in a mission team's prayer vigil on the Tijuana side of the border fence. We placed our hands on those rusty sheets of metal as we prayed. We prayed for forgiveness for having built barriers that obstruct God's vision for nature and for human communities. We prayed for healing of the resentment the fence causes on both sides of the border. We prayed for family members separated by this fence. As a community of vision, our prayers were focused by a common image: the border fence. Yet on that day the ugly metal wall couldn't fence in our prayers, which spilled out in every direction and crossed every artificial boundary.

"Something there is that doesn't love a wall," the poet Robert Frost averred, "That wants it down." Perhaps that something is prayer.

Seeing Signs

Prayer means seeing signs of what God is up to in the world. In the Gospel of John, Jesus changes water into wine (2:1-12), heals a lame man (5:1-18), and feeds a crowd of five thousand with five loaves and two fish (6:1-14). These miracles are considered signs of Jesus' glory, revealing his divine nature. The signs Jesus performs in a compressed moment of time point to what God is doing in the world over a longer period of time: transforming, healing, feeding.

Prayer means paying attention to signs and wonders we notice with the eyes of faith. Sometimes, like the psalmist, we notice signs of God's providential care everywhere we turn:

> You make springs gush forth in the valleys;
>> they flow between the hills,
> giving drink to every wild animal;
>> the wild asses quench their thirst.
> By the streams the birds of the air have their habitation;
>> they sing among the branches.

From your lofty abode you water the mountains;
   the earth is satisfied with the fruit of your work.

You cause the grass to grow for the cattle,
   and plants for people to use,
to bring forth food from the earth,
   and wine to gladden the human heart,
oil to make the face shine,
   and bread to strengthen the human heart

   .   .   .   .

These all look to you
   to give them their food in due season;
when you give to them, they gather it up;
   when you open your hand, they are filled
   with good things. (Psalm 104:13-15, 27-28)

Sometimes prayer focuses attention on small, almost hidden signs. Jesus was fascinated with small things: a lump of leaven, a lost coin, a mustard seed. He once compared the reign of God to the mustard seed, "which, when sown upon the ground, is the smallest of all the seeds on earth; yet when it is sown it grows up and becomes the greatest of all shrubs, and puts forth large branches, so that the birds of the air can make nests in its shade" (Mark 4:30-32). People look to God to work in big, dramatic ways. Yet often the signs of God's body language are so small they go unnoticed. Who would have suspected the lowly mustard seed?

With attentive eyes, people of faith learn to look for mustard-seed-sized signs of God's grandeur. They encounter the world with a sense of great expectation and hope. They don't hoard the secret for themselves but joyfully bring others into the act.

Tom is a church musician who welcomes groups of people—often strangers—to sing together. When Tom was growing up, his mother cultivated a sense of wonder in him. Every morning as he prepared to leave for school, his mother would say, "Tom, God has marvelous things in store for you today. I wonder what they will be."

Tom believed his mother, so he left his house each day with a great sense of anticipation. "I know it sounds a bit strange, but I actually walked around wondering what God was up to in my life each day," Tom admits with a chuckle. "I kept my eyes open for signs of those 'marvelous things' God had in store for me. And that's the invitation I try to extend as I lead people in singing: God has marvelous things in store for you this day. I wonder what they will be."

Sometimes the signs of God's grace are writ large, sometimes small. And sometimes we have to look and then look again to see signs of God's hand in bleak circumstances. Our mission team made several trips to that border fence in Tijuana before we were ready to pray there. At first glance, it seemed like the last place on earth one would look for signs of God's grace. We had to look and then look again to see God's judgment and mercy in that ugly metal wall.

Prayer as Contemplative Action

Emily, a young adult mission volunteer in Thailand, works at a boarding house for orphaned and abandoned kids from the Hill Tribes. "I live among children who do not exist," writes Emily. "In the mornings, I hold their young, weathered hands as we walk down the road to school. After their afternoon bath, I comb lice out of their hair and help the little ones scrub clean their one school uniform. In the evenings, we share rice and fish. Playing, they get scraped and bruised, and I have seen them bleed. We pray together before bed, crossing ourselves in the name of One who knew and loved them before they were born, One who remembers them now. And yet, according to the government, they do not exist."

The Chinese-descended Hill Tribes are "people of the mountains" who have lived along the Thailand-Myanmar border for generations. They have no birth certificates or citizenship cards, and the Thai government assumes no responsibility for their welfare. When adults are discovered, they are thrown in prison as illegal residents. Their children are left homeless and parentless. If not for the boarding house, most of these twenty-eight children would be sold as sex workers.

"I was prepared to see the poverty," Emily continues. "I was ready to live in the gray of the developing world. I brought antibiotics and vitamins, bug repellent and sunscreen. I came knowing how to wipe noses, sing songs, and laugh at myself. But I did not know to prepare, did not know how to prepare, for the emptiness of life among the forgotten, the unclaimed, the abandoned. If a child has no country, no home, no family, no place to go where she belongs and where no one can ask her to leave, who is she? It makes the hand holding, the lice picking, the bleeding, the eating, and the praying matter in a new way. It is in those interactions that they exist, indisputably. It is in those interactions that I too am becoming real."

Emily sees children who, according to legal authorities, do not exist. She knows they exist because she spends her days caring for them. "I have seen them bleed," she states matter-of-factly. And in this simple act of paying attention to them, Emily confirms their very existence—and her own existence as well. This is the power of paying attention, the fertile soil in which prayer is rooted.

Emily shares bedtime prayers with the children. These formal prayers are but explicit moments within Emily's ongoing, implicit contemplation of these children and their world. She beholds them with fierce attention, and does not look away, as many in Thailand do. Because she truly sees these children—sees them as both fragile and blessed—every interaction Emily has with them matters "in a new way" and has real, life-giving significance.

Luke tells of a time when Jesus went to visit his Bethany friends Mary and Martha. As the story goes, Jesus upbraids Martha for being "worried and distracted by many things," while he commends Mary for sitting attentively at his feet and listening to him (Luke 10:38-42). Throughout church history, interpreters have pointed to this passage to extol the contemplative life (Mary) over the active life (Martha). Yet, as we observe in Emily's account, authentic contemplation pays attention to the concrete specifics of daily life. Activity can be undertaken with a deeply contemplative spirit.

Action-grounded prayer complements prayerful action. It's not an either/or but a both/and.

In her compassion for the children who do not exist, Emily embodies both Mary and Martha sensibilities. She offers hospitality to these children and shares life with them, all the while giving them the one thing that is most needful: her attentive eyes—a form of prayer. Prayerful attention is the linchpin that holds contemplative action together.

Prayer Begins with Letting Go

Jesus challenged Martha to let go of her many preoccupations so that she could begin paying attention. Prayer begins with relinquishment, with letting go. You can't have a good conversation with someone when you're preoccupied and your mind is elsewhere. You turn off the TV, unplug the iPod, put your project on standby, and give your undivided attention to the other person. Okay, it's possible to have a good conversation while taking a walk, riding in the car, or fixing a meal together. But in those cases, active listening requires extra effort. Most of us have the attention span of a gnat, and we get easily distracted by random thoughts and memories, unfinished tasks, multitasking, or ubiquitous ads for consumer products. *Drink Coca-Cola.* See?

Poet Mary Oliver doesn't rely on "fancy words" or God-talk when she prays. She begins by letting go of her world of words, so that she can pay close attention to the world right before her eyes:

> It doesn't have to be
> the blue iris, it could be
> weeds in a vacant lot, or a few
> small stones; just
> pay attention, then patch
>
> a few words together and don't try
> to make them elaborate, this isn't
> a contest but the doorway

into thanks, and a silence in which
another voice may speak.

Our hearts may feel more inclined toward gratitude when we behold a beautiful flower ("the blue iris"). Yet every nook and cranny of creation—even pebbles and weeds—can be a "doorway" into prayer if we let go of our preconceptions and simply pay attention. The poet trusts that by rooting our prayer in what we see right before us, with attentive eyes, we put ourselves in a receptive posture, sitting at the feet of Jesus, listening for God's word.

Visualize the Liturgy

I attended a work camp that invited teen participants to share "God sightings" each evening during worship. Teens shared brief, heartfelt testimonies about where they had seen God at work that day. These stories from various work sites helped us see how our individual efforts were connected to God's larger, ongoing story of repairing creation. Throughout that week, however, most of the evening programs were pre-scripted. Indeed, throughout the summer, communities across the country used the identical script for leading worship. Scripts developed to promote ecumenical consistency and reliability from one work camp to the next unfortunately leave the evening liturgy disconnected from the liturgy of the day.

Liturgy means "public service" or "the work of the people." Worship leaders are challenged to shape liturgy that reflects the daily service and work of God's people in the world. Those responsible for planning and coordinating evening worship, for instance, need to ask: *How does the liturgy of the evening flow directly from the liturgy of the day? In what ways will worship provide space for sharing joys and concerns encountered in the field? How can our liturgy reflect this very place we're sojourning, so that participants begin to see the deep connections between their own daily activities and God's saving activity?*

In visualizing the liturgy, the Benedictine motto *ora et labora* ("pray and work") provides guidance. Benedictine brothers don't compartmentalize their daily activities into mundane and sacred spheres. They view their work as integral to the life of faith, not something they must grudgingly grind their way through in order to tend to their spiritual lives. Scrubbing pots and pans can be as prayerful an activity as singing a psalm. Work in the fields can be as sanctifying as communal worship when performed with the purpose of glorifying God.

We're not as proficient as monks in the art of integrating our liturgies of work and prayer. This art, like learning to dance, requires skill. Monks know "the dance steps" as they move gracefully through the day, alternating rhythms of manual labor, communal prayer, and meditation on scripture. (Benedict emphasized *lectio* as well as *ora et labora*.) The rest of us rarely experience all three rhythms during the course of a single day. For us, worship offers a break from work; work happens at a remove from worship; and Bible study is something else altogether. We don't quite know the dance steps, so we move a bit awkwardly from one activity to the other. But we can learn to dance.

For mission-trip leaders, visualizing the liturgy involves choreography, paying attention to how our bodies move through the day. Attentive eyes constantly look for ways to help team members move more gracefully between the rhythms of *ora et labora et lectio*. We'll explore these rhythms in more detail in the following chapters.

For the Journey

Recruit volunteers from your mission team for the following roles that involve seeing with attentive eyes:

- Photographer/Videographer—takes pictures to document the trip

- Historian/Griot/Bard/Minstrel—tells stories about the places your team visits

- Liturgy Crafter—looks for ways to integrate daily liturgies of work and prayer

- Journal Keeper—maintains the team journal to which any team member may contribute daily entries

- Scrapbook Keeper—creates and keeps track of scrapbook from sending congregation (shared informally with local hosts)

The following reflection prompts for journal and discussion encourage paying attention while on the road:

- How did you see God at work today?

- Where did you hear the gospel proclaimed today?

- What kinds of poverty did you see today?

- What gifts and assets did you encounter within the community today?

- When did you experience failure or when were you discouraged today?

- What signs of hope did you see today?

- Where did you see hospitality offered/received today?

- What visual image today will always stay with you?

During your trip, gather your group for contemplative prayer. Invite participants to close their eyes, visualize the flow of their day, and focus silently on one particular object that stands out for them. Then read aloud the Mary Oliver poem "Praying" (quoted in this chapter). Invite the group to let their focal objects become a "doorway into thanks." Allow a period of silence, followed by shared spoken prayer.

Invite your congregation to pray each day for a team member. Provide devotional guides so that all parishioners can follow your itinerary and lift your mission team in prayer each day. For an example, see *A Daily Devotional for the Kenya Mission Team and Friends*, prepared by Pastors Carolyn and Bruce Gillette for Limestone Presbyterian Church (Wilmington, Delaware): www.limestonepres byterian.org/KenyaTripDevotional.htm.

During and after your trip, reflect on Henri Nouwen's insight from his journal *¡Gracias!*:

> Living with the poor does not keep me away from evil, but it does allow me to see evil in sharper, clearer ways. It does not lead me automatically to the good either, but will help me see good in a brighter light, less hidden and more convincing.

In what ways does Nouwen's observation illumine your own outreach experience? What is it about poverty that casts good and evil into bolder relief?

If partnering with a host group, try the photo comparison activity pioneered by University Presbyterian Church of Austin, as described in this chapter.

Some places have few mirrors, so digital cameras can give people a chance to see themselves, provided they grant permission for their photo to be taken. When feasible, digital photos can be uploaded to a Web site during the mission trip. Good photos are a boon to telling the story of a mission trip. Ask a tech-savvy member of your team to create a mission-trip slide show with soundtrack on DVD.

Invite your mission team to map its journey before going on a trip. There are many ways to make a map, so plan this as a fun learning activity for your group. Then after the trip, map the new field of relationships you have experienced. Note ways in which the trip changed perceptions. Display "before" and "after" maps for others to see.

Praise the LORD!

Praise God in his sanctuary;

praise him in his mighty firmament!

Praise God for his mighty deeds;

praise him according to his surpassing greatness!

Praise God with trumpet sound;

praise him with lute and harp!

Praise God with tambourine and dance;

praise him with strings and pipe!

Praise God with clanging cymbals;

praise him with loud clashing cymbals!

Let everything that breathes praise the LORD!

Praise the LORD! (Ps. 150, adapted)

Maker of creation's choir,

you sing the Song of Love to us.

Breathe your Spirit into our singing

until the rhythm of your mercy

shapes all our music-making

and we join with one another to

give you thanks and praise.

Amen.

—*Susan Briehl*

4
Attuned Ears

The sign out front said "Westminster Presbyterian Church," but the scene looked more like a lumberyard with piles of two-by-fours, stacks of composite board sheets, ladders and scaffolding scattered about. This Gulfport, Mississippi, church building survived Katrina relatively unscathed, so members immediately converted the whole campus into a relief center. Several members even moved into FEMA trailers on the church grounds. From there they coordinated the steady streams of volunteers assisting with this long-term relief effort. Seven months after the storm, the Gulf Coast was still littered with debris and roofless houses.

I was with a mission team of twenty-five teens and seven adults from Hinsdale, a western suburb of Chicago. Each day most of us helped with roof repair, working alongside groups from across the country. Each evening, those of us staying at Westminster gathered in the sanctuary after dinner for singing and worship. We totaled seventy-five teenagers, thirty adults, and a dozen younger children, mostly from Presbyterian and United Church of Christ congregations. The song leader, probably in his early twenties, stood before us with wavy red hair and cheerful smile, his trusty guitar strapped over his shoulder. Sam hailed from Florida and enjoyed playing for youth events, eagerly strumming "Awesome God" and other standard praise songs. Lyrics were projected on a screen so we could lift our voices together as we worshiped.

That first evening we sang only upbeat songs extolling God's grandeur and Jesus' sacrificial love. I found myself longing for another melody, something that would connect our hearts more intimately to the relief work we had spent the whole day doing: pounding nails, cleaning up debris, caring for abandoned pets, listening to the stories of displaced people. "Wade in the Water" came to mind, as Gulf Coast residents had literally waded through water from the powerful storm surge. They were still wading through a sea of red tape trying to get government aid and insurance claims processed. "By the Waters of Babylon" would have been a fitting psalm to sing as a simple round. And the spiritual "There Is a Balm in Gilead" could have offered healing and comfort to those who "sometimes feel discouraged and think their work's in vain."

All three of these songs were included in the Presbyterian hymnal standing in the pew racks before us. Several of us wondered about expanding our music repertoire, so we approached Sam to thank him for his leadership and ask whether we might sing some "alternative songs" as well during the week. Sam politely demurred, saying he didn't know those songs and thought the youth would prefer the more familiar praise music. So every evening we sang "Awesome God," while my soul yearned for songs in a minor key, tunes that would travel with me back to the work site the following day.

I experienced similar yearning during a weeklong work camp in northern Indiana. The work camp orchestrated almost fifty work sites throughout the community. Most focused on residential home repair, painting house exteriors and fixing dilapidated steps and porches. Once again the songs at evening worship seemed to be standard youth-rally fare. They didn't attune our ears to the sounds of outreach offered throughout the day. Whatever happened to "If I Had a Hammer" I wondered. That song would weave our work into a larger fabric of justice seeking, and it could be sung creatively—to a reggae beat, for instance. Worship planners preferred praise music because most youth attending were familiar with these songs, and singing them together would help strangers bond more quickly. Songs were also selected to deepen individuals' personal relationship with Jesus. While that is a worthy goal, Christian music must cover a more expansive landscape to enliven the life of faith.

Living the Psalm-Shaped Life

If we hope to draw nearer to Jesus, we need to learn to sing like Jesus. As a faithful Jew, Jesus chanted and sang the Psalms. The Psalter was his primary songbook and prayer book. In commenting on "the secret of the Psalter," German martyr Dietrich Bonhoeffer notes that we come before God using the very prayers Jesus himself prayed. "Jesus prayed the Psalter," Bonhoeffer writes, "and now it has become his prayer for all time." Indeed, Bonhoeffer claims that Jesus continues praying those very psalms for his church, even those troublesome psalms we find it difficult to pray or sing with our own lips (such as Ps. 137:7-9).

Worship in Jesus' name attunes our ears to the language, imagery, and emotional range of the Psalms. We can sing songs that resonate with Psalm 150, praising God with every available musical instrument and with dance simply because of God's majesty. Yet we need to balance those songs with ones that echo Psalm 146, praising the creator God who "keeps faith forever ... executes justice for the oppressed ... gives food to the hungry ... sets the prisoners free ... opens the eyes of the blind ... lifts up those who are bowed down ... watches over the strangers ... upholds the orphan and the widow." And we also need songs with lyrics of lament, such as in Psalm 6:6: "I grow weary because of my groaning; every night I drench my pillow and flood my bed with tears" (ELW). When we sing only praise songs we are in danger of perpetually congratulating God and ourselves on the way things are aligned in this world. We are like those whose "boundaries enclose a pleasant land" and who have been blessed by "a rich inheritance" (Ps. 16:6, ELW). These songs endorse the status quo. They don't open our ears to hear how God is on the side of the poor and downtrodden, contesting all powers and principalities that keep them oppressed.

Ethel Johnson, a church worker and veteran of the Civil Rights movement, was once asked by a teenager if it's okay to be angry with God. Ethel replied in slow, measured cadence: "I could not have lived to be a seventy-four-year-old black woman in this country without getting fed up with God on a regular basis. But you know what? It's okay for me to be angry with God, because God and I have a long-term relationship, and God can handle my anger. And in my Bible, I read the Psalms, and they give me a language for my anger."

Ethel Johnson delights in singing praises to God. But her soul also needs to sing of injustice and grief. Her ears are attuned to these ever-present realities—not only in this country but in Nigeria, where she serves in mission several months of each year. As a follower of Jesus, Ethel lives a psalm-shaped life and helps others strive to do the same.

Tuning In

How can we attune our ears to what's around us if we're tuned in elsewhere? With the prevalence of communications technology, this is an issue not only for teens but for adults as well. Two popular devices that dislocate us from our immediate surroundings are the cell phone and the iPod (or any portable music player). The cell phone speaks to our need for *intimacy*, for staying connected with close friends and family regardless of distance. The iPod speaks to our need for *fidelity* by playing favorite songs, music we can count on to be there for us at our beck and call.

Both the cell phone and iPod appeal to personal preference and allow us to distance ourselves from the environment at hand. Instead of paying attention to the sounds in my environment—which may be unpleasant or annoying—I summon a familiar sound track for my life, high fidelity music instantly available. Instead of sharing conversation and life with people in this place, I talk with or text-message someone in a distant place.

Communication devices invite users to be in more than one place at a time. That's why wise mission-team leaders set guidelines about permissible devices to take on a trip. Many groups ban iPods and cell phones by making the following appeal: "We're using common transportation (van, bus, airplane), so while on the road we also need to converse with fellow team members and listen to common music. This will keep us focused on one another and strengthen our fellowship. And this will open us to pay more attention to the folks we're going to serve."

Expect push-back if you take this approach! And not just from teens. On a youth-adult mission trip, parents back home want to stay connected to their kids via cell phone. They don't understand why this could cause problems for the group. Assuming you'll be somewhere that gets a satellite signal, assure anxious parents that several leaders will carry cell phones and will relay messages home during the trip. Updates sent to an e-mail list or posted on a Web site are convenient ways to keep folks informed without a steady stream of phone calls interrupting the new community being formed.

Saying Yes Before Saying No

The practice of honoring the body is affirmation before it is admonition. In other words, saying yes to God's good gift precedes saying no to whatever disrespects that gift. One says yes to keeping sabbath before saying no to shopping on Sundays, for instance. A mission team therefore needs to say yes to group songs for the road before saying no to personal portable music players. Here are two examples.

A mission team from Hopewell, New Jersey, travels to Dunkirk, New York, to convert a former creamery into a downtown church. One mission-team member composes a theme song for the trip: "Send Us Out Two by Two," based on Mark 6:7-13. The group sings the song in worship as they are commissioned to serve. The congregation joins in singing the refrain. As mission-team members and their families gather to board vans and pray for travel mercies, they sing the song again. Every day they sing the song for morning devotions. They sing the song at a picnic with coworkers in Dunkirk. When they return to Hopewell and share testimonies of their trip in worship, they sing the song yet again. "Send Us Out" has become a sound track for their lives while on the road.

A youth-and-adult mission team from North Carolina learns several songs in Spanish to sing with our church partner in Guatemala. The songs include "Yo Tengo Gozo"—"I've got that joy . . . down in my heart." "Yo Tengo" is easy to learn, even for most of our team members who are not Spanish speakers. We sing the song at each pre-trip gathering, including a fund-raising dinner and commissioning service.

On our first night in Guatemala we gather for worship and fellowship with the Coatepeque congregation. In broken Spanish we each in turn introduce ourselves by stating our name and one interesting fact about us. My son says his name, then attempts to say his age (*Yo tengo quince años.*) but omits the tilda for *años*. So instead of saying, "I have fifteen years," he states that he has fifteen anatomical features on his posterior—prompting much laughter and not a little embarrassment for my son.

As a perfect face-saving segue, we all launch into singing "Yo Tengo Gozo." Sharing one of the Guatemalans' favorite songs produces an immediate bond between our two groups. Our Guatemalan friends sing it a bit differently than we learned it, but we quickly adjust and sing "Yo Tengo" with gusto every time we gather.

Singing with Ears Wide Open

My colleague Susan Briehl observes that

> singing makes us vulnerable; singing together makes us vulnerable with and to one another, including the stranger. And when the music is new, or the rhythm, style, or form of

accompaniment is unfamiliar, the vulnerability increases. Perhaps at this point of vulnerability our witness to and embodiment of Christ, the Vulnerable One, becomes most visible. When we are vulnerable—but not afraid of being destroyed—we can envision a world with fewer walls and divisions.

For many years I've sung in a church choir. Weekly rehearsals render me vulnerable because I don't read music well—plenty of opportunities to be exposed. I'm grateful for the support of choristers who can nail the notes even on a first sing-through. And over the years I've learned to listen closely, not just to my fellow tenors but to the whole ensemble. Just as tasting is mostly a matter of smell, singing is mostly a matter of listening, attuning one's ears. I constantly adjust pitch, volume, and tempo by listening to the group (and occasionally watching the conductor's cues!). I enjoy the sheer physicality of singing a spiritual or gospel hymn when we're out of our music folders and blending voices together with precision and power.

Our fundamental medium in Christian worship is "sounding bodies," vibrating bodies, bodies alive with the words and music of prayer and praise, proclamation and sacramental sign. "Singing helps knit the story of God's mercy into our bones," Susan says. "And those words, that music, our bodies, and this assembly all have the capacity to bear the living presence of the Word of God to us and to the world. . . . Perhaps in worship—whether using chants from Taizé, African American spirituals, or Euro-American hymns, whether accompanied by drum, piano, or organ, or sung a cappella, whether learned 'by ear' through call and response or sung from hymnbooks—we sing ourselves into being the Body of Christ."

Hearing a New Song

As a team member of United Methodist young adults, Matt traveled to Senegal to meet Methodist young adults from that country. In Senegal Matt heard all kinds of new sounds. The sound of worship was different. People sang traditional United Methodist hymns, only recomposed to calypso and reggae rhythms. And everywhere his group traveled, they were accompanied by djembe drums. "This is a culture that loves to sing," Matt notes, "and the music of Senegalese Christians is driven and carried by rhythms."

The sounds Matt most vividly remembers, however, arose out of the dominant Muslim culture: "Every morning I arose at dawn with the sound of morning prayers over a loudspeaker. Soon the whole city would burst with the sounds of people talking, horse-drawn buggies, and clanky automobiles. In Senegal, the rhythm of life is determined by five periods of prayer."

One afternoon his group was traveling by foot through the downtown area of the capital city when suddenly men everywhere were laying down their mats for prayer, and all became quiet—except, of course, for the Americans who continued conversing. "One of our Senegalese brothers kindly pointed out to us that we should respect the prayer time. In our silence, I looked around and saw that the entire city had ceased activity. Traffic stopped right where it was. Our bus was right down the road and yet not moving because the driver was in prayer. And then the prayers began to be called out and the men were in a whole new rhythm of prayer, until finally it was over, and like magic, the entire city came back to life. It was unbelievable."

Matt admires how Muslim prayer has shaped a way of life for the people of Senegal—including the Christian community, who bow in silent respect with their Muslim neighbors. Matt's brother in Christ coached him to attune his ears to the sounds of grace, spoken in an unfamiliar language and in a land far from home. Matt and his companions learned that day how the body of Christ honors the body of a kindred spirit. They are indeed following in the footsteps of One who himself got coaching once in ear attunement.

According to Matthew 15, when a Canaanite woman begs Jesus to heal her daughter, he first ignores her. He doesn't say a word. Then Jesus rejects her as a Gentile, a nonbeliever ("I was sent only to the lost sheep of the house of Israel.") And finally, he insults this woman by calling her a "dog" ("It is not fair to take the children's food and throw it to the dogs.") The woman refuses to be humiliated, and uses the dog analogy to her advantage: "Yes, Lord, yet even the dogs eat the crumbs that fall from their masters' table." If mealtimes around her table are merciful, surely Jesus can spare some crumbs of mercy for her sick daughter.

Perhaps it's the look in her determined eyes, perhaps the persistence in her voice. Whatever it was, Jesus has a change of heart that day. Jesus begins to imagine that his circle of ministry—and indeed the great mercy of God—are wider than even he had known before. Attuning his ears to this Gentile woman's voice, Jesus hears the theme of a new song. He hears God summon him to a broader, more inclusive ministry. A ministry that extends the table until there is finally room enough and food enough for everyone.

> O sing to the LORD a new song;
>   sing to the LORD, all the earth.
> Sing to the LORD, bless his name;
>   tell of his salvation from day to day. (Ps. 96:1-2)

For the Journey

Gather a group of attentive listeners who will commit to hearing the stories of mission-team members when they return from their trip. Arrange for this group to meet with your mission team before you leave, perhaps over a meal. Pair up for guided conversation, sharing stories about life experience (for example, favorite songs, hymns, or music) and swapping travel tales in particular (a time you experienced hospitality while on the road, for instance).

Perform a comic skit to dramatize how communication devices such as phones, computers, and iPods dislocate us from the place where we find ourselves. Role-play a group trying to hold a conversation while being constantly interrupted by ringing cell phones, halfway heard by someone Instant Messaging, and completely ignored by an iPod user. Then role-play how attentive conversation might occur when all are less distracted and more present to one another.

Make a sound track for the road. Include songs by Bread for the Journey, especially from *Global Songs 1, 2,* and *3* (see www.bfjmusic .com for CDs and songbooks). Add new songs to your sound track while on the road.

Visit www.npr.org/templates/story /story.php?storyId=5419893 and listen to the story of Peter Spring, a piano tuner who traveled from Oregon to New Orleans to help with the Katrina relief effort by offering his talents:

Spring was in large part motivated by personal loss: the death of his son four years earlier caused by cancer. "I'm a third responder. I'm not interested in danger . . . I'm not here to clean up . . . ; I'm here for morale. . . . It does help when people here find out about the depth and the quality of my loss. . . . It helps them understand and believe that I'm not here to take anything from them, to get anything from them. I came down because I know about loss." Discuss how Spring attuned his ears for outreach.

Ask the group to compare the God imagery in Psalm 150 and Psalm 146 (provide handouts). Circle phrases that describe God's creative and saving activity in the world, the reasons why we praise and glorify God. How does each psalm attune our ears differently to God's activity in this world? Which psalm attunes our ears more acutely to God's grace and mercy for our sake? How does your group's song repertoire reflect this balance?

Learn this hymn to sing throughout your trip. Use the suggested tune (see *Presbyterian Hymnal*, No. 432) or an alternate tune with similar meter.

GOD, YOU LOVE THE WORLD!

A Hymn of Dedication Before a Mission Trip

God, you love the world! You sent your only Son,
And you said, "Go share my love with everyone."
So we seek to serve you in our homes and towns,
And we work to show the world: Your love abounds!

Refrain
Lead us, as we go this day;
Guide us as we work and pray.
Give us, when each day is through,
True joy, found in serving you.

By your Spirit, some build houses, safe and strong,
Some are called to share your Word in prayer and song.
Some are called to heal the sick and fight disease,
Some are called to save the land by planting trees.
Refrain

Teach us that in loving, we must listen well.
Help us hear the stories others have to tell.
Help us learn from other people and their ways.
May we be united as we offer praise.
Refrain

John 3:16-1; Tune: Argentine folk melody
ARGENTINA 11.11.11.11 refrain "Song of Hope"

As we venture forth

to serve in your name, O God,
May your strong hand rest upon our shoulder
guiding, admonishing, encouraging,
and may the wisdom of all eyes be our sight.

Help us hold possessions lightly
and faith firmly,
trusting in you to provide
our daily bread,
safe lodging,
a gracious host.

Merciful God, convert our appetite for stuff
to hunger for justice
that rolls down like waters
and righteousness
like an ever-flowing stream.

May the wisdom of all eyes be our sight.

May our ears gather up the voice of your Spirit.

—Lani Wright

5
Sturdy Backs

How do you pack your bags for a trip? Some travelers "don't leave home without it." They pack everything but the kitchen sink. Personally I wouldn't want to drag around all that extra stuff—hard on the lower back. I refrain from ridicule, though, because when I'm miles from the nearest superstore, I'm glad to have a pack rat as a traveling companion. Need extra batteries? Pepto-Bismol? a complete socket-wrench set? These are your go-to guys.

I usually ponder what to pack when preparing for a trip. Ponder means "to weigh," an apt description of how I assess each item before it goes in the bag. Will I be staying in a hotel? If so, no need to pack soap, shampoo, or bedding. Will I be visiting family or friends? I can always borrow an extra jacket or an umbrella. My goal is to pack only what's essential for the trip.

While on the road, I don't like to be too weighed down, encumbered by lots of stuff I don't need or won't be using. The lighter my backpack, the lighter my spirit. While on the road, I'm free from the claims made by fifty years of accumulated stuff: stacks of books and journals that beckon to be read; children's outgrown clothing that needs sorting and donating; even unopened boxes from the last move. I enjoy taking a vacation from my stuff, and it usually gets along just fine without me too, except for the houseplants, which my neighbors kindly water.

When preparing for a mission trip, I ponder less and rely more on team leaders to provide an itemized packing list. I trust leaders to recommend items based on safety, comfort, and decorum. This is not the time, I've learned, to make a personal fashion statement! Making sure I have the right stuff in my backpack gives me a sense of security and confidence, especially when I venture to unfamiliar places.

Traveling Light in Guatemala

Several years ago I bought a new duffel bag for a ten-day mission trip to Guatemala. I bought an identical blue bag for my fifteen-year-old son Jonathan. We carefully packed our respective bags with hats, gloves, work boots, mosquito netting, flashlights, first aid kit, toiletries, permethrin-saturated clothing, deep woods insect repellent, and gift items for our host family. Even though our bags were bulging, we complied with that time-honored rule of the road: bring only what you can carry by yourself.

The day we embarked on our trip, a flight delay caused our mission team to miss a connecting flight, and we had to spend the night in Miami. The airline *assured* us that our sixteen duffel bags would be transferred aboard our early-morning flight to Guatemala City. You can guess what happened next. We landed in Guatemala to discover that all our carefully packed bags were still sitting in the Miami airport.

Our mission team needed to get under way, so one member stayed at the airport, while the other fifteen set off with day packs. "Traveling light" indeed! We were eager for a change of clothes but not anxious, confident that our bags would soon catch up to us. When the bags did arrive three days later, we flocked to the delivery van to claim our belongings. Well, most of us claimed our belongings. The only blue duffel bag on the van belonged to Jonathan. My own carefully packed, identical blue bag had been lost or stolen in transit.

You know those moments when you get that sudden sinking feeling? When the ground beneath your feet begins to shift—and you're not standing on a moving sidewalk? For me, this was one of those moments.

Before realizing that my bag had "gone missing," I was feeling safe and secure, even in this faraway land. Faced with the sudden loss of all my clothing and equipment, I now seemed strangely lost myself. Without my sure supply of stuff at hand, I felt vulnerable and exposed. What would I wear each day? How would I protect my body from the blazing sun, frequent downpours, swarms of disease-bearing insects? How would I equip myself for work and play, for worship and fellowship with the Jerusalem Church, our partner congregation in Coatepeque?

Beyond these concerns for personal well-being, I was acutely aware of how my lost bag would burden other mission-team members and our Guatemalan hosts. I knew I'd have to rely on the mercy of traveling companions and the kindness of strangers throughout our stay. The small, resilient Jerusalem Church was already stretching limited resources to accommodate our group. And now they'd have to clothe me as well. This further imposition didn't seem fair to anyone.

Being Prepared

In Mark 6:7-13, Jesus commissions twelve disciples and sends them out two-by-two among the villages to minister in his name. "He ordered them to take nothing for their journey except a staff; no bread, no bag, no money in their belts; but to wear sandals and not to put on two tunics" (vv. 8-9). The disciples, it seems, were expected to travel *very* light and to depend on the hospitality of local folk to meet their basic needs for food and shelter. Jesus was evidently *not* schooled in the Boy Scout motto "Be Prepared."

But perhaps Jesus had in mind a different way of being prepared. Perhaps the most challenging preparation is that of the heart. For when our hearts are preoccupied with all the *things* we're toting in our backpacks, with what we're wearing, with the souvenirs we plan to buy, and with all the things we're holding in our hands—even the gifts we're bringing—why then, it's hard to be present with compassion to the people we've come to visit and serve.

How humbling it is to stand before others with no possessions, wearing no badge of entitlement or wardrobe of privilege.

Our mission-team leaders viewed my loss as a teachable moment, though not at my personal expense. They didn't put me on display as an object lesson of Mark 6. Nor did they downplay the importance of my missing stuff. They acknowledged what mattered to me and commiserated with me as fellow travelers, walking with me in my (absent) shoes. Word went out within the Jerusalem Church that one of the American guests needed to be clothed. Within hours, trousers, shirts, shoes, socks, and toiletries had been collected and brought to me in a suitcase. I didn't get everything I had originally packed, yet I got everything I needed for my stay. I, who had come many miles to serve, was now being clothed with compassion by fellow travelers and generous hosts.

Leaders did not regard my lost bag as a technical challenge to solve by applying current know-how. They viewed the situation as an adaptive challenge for the whole mission team as well as for the Jerusalem Church. They did not say, "We'll take charge and fix your problem." Instead they announced, "Our brother has lost his belongings. How can we come to his aid?" This rallied the energy and resourcefulness of the group. It inspired them to take collective responsibility for meeting this challenge. And it set the tone for addressing other adaptive challenges we were to face during our days in Guatemala. (See earlier discussion of this subject in chapter 2, "Preparing to Lead.")

Planting Good Seed

I thought of Jesus' disciples as I reckoned with lost luggage in Guatemala. They too entered villages where people were struggling to make ends meet. Instead of showing up with a bag of ready-made solutions and a take-charge attitude, disciple teams arrived with open hands ready to receive, open hearts prepared to stand in solidarity with their hosts. This must have felt risky to those newly minted disciples and slightly bewildering to those who took them in. Yet by traveling light, disciples and their hosts were able to shift perspective from glass-half-empty to glass-half-full. And together, they accomplished marvelous works in Jesus' name.

Coming from positions of privilege, we tend to view the Two-Thirds World from a glass-half-empty perspective. We survey the scene and see mostly problems and predicaments. We don't tend to notice a community's strengths and assets. We need to unload the glass-half-empty frame of reference from our backpacks and set it aside. Instead, we can ask, "What unique gifts has God given these people? What charisms are present in this community? What signs of God's abundance are already evident in this place?"

> *We need to unload the glass-half-empty frame of reference from our backpacks and set it aside.*

In her haunting novel *The Poisonwood Bible*, Barbara Kingsolver portrays this contrast between glass-half-empty and glass-half-full approaches to mission. Kingsolver introduces us to Nathan Price, a self-appointed missionary who takes his wife and four daughters into the heart of the Belgian Congo in 1959. Determined to bring the Light of the World to "the people of this dark continent," Nathan doesn't pause long enough to get to know these people or to learn their language and their customs, let alone their spiritual beliefs. Nathan is convinced that he'll simply scatter gospel seeds through sound biblical preaching, then sit back and watch his ministry take root, blossom, and flourish.

Believing the Congo to be a godless, glass-half-empty place, Nathan brings along bags of literal as well as figurative seed. He doesn't realize that seeds must be planted in mounds instead of in rows to withstand the torrential rains of the Congo. The locals kindly replant his garden, though Nathan won't accept their wisdom; he indignantly levels the hills back into rows. The first heavy rain naturally washes the seed away. Even when he learns to plant correctly, Nathan's squash, beans, and pumpkin seed are useless because they lack pollinators—"a world of bugs who have no idea what to do with a Kentucky wonder bean."

Meanwhile, Nathan Price's preaching is a disaster. He brings no good news for these people, only words of judgment. "Nathan" is the Hebrew word for "gift," yet this gift comes with a "Price" tag attached. In contrast to Nathan Price stands Brother Fowles, the former missionary to this village. Nathan's teenage daughter muses that this kindly old man looks like Santa Claus. Indeed, Brother Fowles arrives bearing a bagful of gifts for her entire family.

Brother Fowles has a glass-half-full view of the villagers' spiritual life. He explains to a skeptical Nathan Price that they are "very religious people."

> Everything they do is with one eye to the spirit. When they plant their yams and manioc, they're praying. When they harvest, they're praying. Even when they conceive their children, I think they're praying. . . . I think the Congolese have a world of God's grace in their lives, along with a dose of hardship that can kill a person entirely. I happen to think they already knew how to make a joyful noise unto the Lord a long time ago. . . . Have you heard the songs they sing here in Kilanga? . . . They're very worshipful. It's a grand way to begin a church service, singing a Congolese hymn to the rainfall on the seed yams. It's quite easy to move from there to the parable of the mustard seed. Many parts of the Bible make good sense here, if only you change a few words.

Who's Serving Whom?

Brother Fowles goes out on a limb, so to speak, when he challenges Nathan Price's interpretive frame for Romans 11: "Brother Price, . . . don't you sometimes think about this, as you share the food of your Congolese brethren and gladden your heart with their songs? Do you get the notion we are the branch that's grafted on here, sharing in the richness of these African roots?" Brother Fowles echoes a sentiment we often hear from mission-team veterans: "I received far more than I gave." Perhaps this is how it ought to be. For inviting others to give of their time, talents, and treasure is one of the most humanizing gestures we can offer.

Each March my sister Judy sends me a birthday card stuffed with a wad of one-dollar bills. Judy, who has Down syndrome, is paid $2 a day for laboring in a sheltered workshop. When she's in a good mood, Judy usually sends me a full week's wages. So my sense of fair play tells me to keep a few dollars and tactfully return the rest. I shouldn't take advantage of Judy's generosity and allow her to give away so much of her hard-earned money. Besides, she needs to save up her dollars for that dream vacation to California she hopes to take one day! I've come to realize, however, that extravagant giving brings life-enhancing joy to Judy, and so my obligation is to receive her gift with a grateful heart.

One of the most important faith lessons we learn on our trips, however, is how to receive hospitality and gifts from others.

One October our church youth group decided to trick-or-treat on behalf of the local food pantry. We went door-to-door throughout the neighborhood, collecting baskets full of canned and dry goods. The teens paused before approaching a house at the end of one street. "We shouldn't go to that house," Sarah said. "Why not?" I asked. "Because that family *gets* food from the pantry at least once a week. It wouldn't be right to ask them to donate." I told them the story of my sister Judy, then asked what they thought about inviting the family to donate. "I think we should ask them," several said. So we did, and the family gave generously. They knew just which food items would be most appreciated!

We carry the expectation of providing charity to others in our mission-trip "backpacks." One of the most important faith lessons we learn on our trips, however, is how to receive hospitality and gifts from others. Jesus calls everyone to follow and serve him as a disciple. In his name, we extend this call to serve to everyone we accompany in mission, whatever that person's social status or means may be.

Faithful Ambassadors

We go forth in mission as ambassadors of the gospel. We also go as ambassadors of our culture. Nathan Price typifies the missionary who conflates these roles, believing that being an ambassador of the gospel means the same thing as being an ambassador of "the American Way." As his story unfolds, we see the consequences of assuming that the gospel can only wear one cultural outfit. The gospel is a clotheshorse, however, and wants to try on the clothing of every culture and transform it.

We go forth in mission as ambassadors of the gospel. We also go as ambassadors of our culture.

Some people have issues with being ambassadors from the U.S.A., especially given our recent military exploits. At times I've felt uncomfortable traveling to other lands, as if wearing the emblem of empire on my shoulders like a Roman soldier from days of yore. In light of the "ugly American" syndrome, one of the unexpected gifts we can receive on a mission trip is reconstructed patriotism.

While in Guatemala, our North Carolina mission team intended to observe the Fourth of July like any other day. Given our country's shameful treatment of Guatemalans in years past, we didn't plan on celebrating Independence Day in their backyard. And yet they planned a wonderful celebration for us: a special meal for dinner with a star-spangled cake, a worship service that gave thanks to God for both of our countries. One of our team processed in with the flag of Guatemala. One of their members processed in with "Old Glory." Right there in the sanctuary. It was a glory-filled occasion indeed.

We no longer felt ashamed to be Americans in that place.

Through my own tears, I could see tears of pride in the eyes of my fifteen-year-old son. My son has felt alienated from this country because of our government's behavior in recent years. Yet it was okay to be patriotic on this night, and in this way. It was a gift of friendship, not an emblem of empire. When the worship service was over, we all piled out into the courtyard to light sparklers and—of all things—Roman candles!

For the Journey

As a leader, you will be advising team members about what to bring and what not to bring. As you present rules and guidelines, consider this an opening to reflect more broadly on our relationship to stuff, especially as North Americans. In what ways are we attached to our stuff, even defined by it? What stuff can we "just not manage without" on our trip? What stuff do we grieve to leave behind? For reference, see the chapter and leader's guide section on "Stuff" in *Way to Live*.

Hold a mock fashion show in which participants contrast appropriate and inappropriate attire for your trip. Mission-team members may bellyache about what they're not allowed to wear. Consider this an opening to discuss our attachment to clothes, our obsession with brands, and ways that clothing invites us to honor the body—or not.

While on the road, what stuff seems most valuable—perhaps something we didn't anticipate? What stuff weighs us down as we travel? What stuff did we bring but now realize we don't need?

Strategize how to counter and subvert consumerism at every turn. Find ways to enlist folks as creators and not just consumers of culture. For example, don't prepackage the experience for your group. Invite team members to design a mission-trip T-shirt during or after the trip.

When a mission-team member breaks or loses something on the road, commiserate but don't pontificate. Don't minimize significance or throw Mark 6 in the person's face right away. Affirm feelings prompted by the loss. Pray for God to protect and defend, and pray for discernment; offer a silent prayer, and if fitting, a shared prayer within the group. Address whatever immediate needs the loss presents, allowing the lesson of the loss to emerge organically over time. Then invite group reflection on this and other losses by asking: "What are our losses teaching us about ourselves and our faith? How have they influenced our relationship to one another? to our hosts?"

Set our feet moving, *O God.*

Guide our feet as we

walk with neighbors near and far,

share common, holy ground that bids us shed our shoes,

tiptoe through green pastures and stroll beside still waters,

trudge up mountainsides with swollen, sweaty feet

to preach peace and shout salvation

stampede for justice

stomp and clap when right prevails

run the good race even when it doesn't

stand with others in the need of prayer

at daybreak and dusk

traversing every threshold

by dance or limp.

Set our feet moving, O God.

Teach us to follow in your footsteps

as we behold those beautiful, bruised feet

that bear our burdens.

Bless our stumblings

and bring us safely to shore.

We pray in Jesus' name and for his sake.

—Don C. Richter

6
Beautiful Feet

Every Wednesday night from November through March, on my way to choir, I meet a cheerful group of volunteers who staff the foot clinic at our church's night shelter for homeless men. Night shelter guests spend long hours each day outdoors on their feet, working or looking for work, in ill-fitting, poorly conditioned shoes, often in cold, rainy weather. The foot clinic offers a warm-water soak for tired, sore feet. Volunteers clip nails, scrape dry and calloused skin, treat infections, bandage cuts, and get to know each guest as they give gentle foot massages. Teenagers as well as adults regularly serve with this outreach ministry.

Grace, one of the teen volunteers, told me this about her experience at the foot clinic:

> I've been serving for five years, ever since I was confirmed. I come every week during the night shelter season, usually with my mom. The foot clinic helps me meet people I share the city with, people I wouldn't get to know otherwise. You get to know some of the regular guys by name; it's like getting a new family.
>
> When I first started it was a bit scary, but then I learned to relax and make the guests feel comfortable while I'm working on their feet. I ask them to tell me about their day, and then I just listen and try to be open to what they share

with me. Sometimes they talk about their struggles with faith. Once I met a guy who was going through a really hard time. He asked me for advice, as though we were already friends.

You can tell the first-timers by the way they sit in the chair. They'll ask, "How old are you? Are you sure you know what you're doing?" Feet are sensitive, and they want to make sure I won't cut them. It's a huge trust thing.

I asked Grace how caring for others' feet affects her view of the world. She said that she pays more attention to feet, though usually subconsciously: "I'll catch myself staring at someone's feet, wondering what they might need. I'll pass by the foot care section at the pharmacy and realize, hey, I know what those things are for! I notice my own feet when I'm drying them and think about all the feet I've dried over the years. And when I get a pedicure, I'm aware of how different it is from the foot clinic. It's the same action but without the trust level."

For Grace, taking the street-worn feet of homeless men in her hands is an act of genuine humility. *Humility* derives from *humus*, the Latin word for "dirt." Feet literally ground the body, connecting it directly to the dirt. The foot clinic grounds Grace in reality and helps her pay attention to things the rest of us might miss. She sees fragile feet that the world ignores. As she bathes them, Grace regards those vulnerable feet as blessed and beautiful, restoring dignity to the whole body belonging to those feet. For Grace and for those who minister with her, washing feet is an act of genuine humanity.

Jesus' Feet

According to the Gospel of John, Jesus' close friend Mary anoints his feet with costly nard, preparing those beautiful feet for the injury they would soon suffer on the Cross (John 12:1-8). This is an intimate gesture, an extravagant act of tender care. Judas Iscariot does not pay attention to Jesus' body—much less his feet; nor does he see

Mary's act as compassionate. Smelling the fragrance, Judas turns up his nose at Mary for *lacking* compassion. "Why didn't you sell that perfume and give the money to the poor?" Judas sniffs. Lacking Mary's humanity and humility, Judas does not look with eyes of faith to see what is unfolding.

Shortly after his own feet have been cared for, Jesus washes disciples' dusty feet during the Last Supper. By washing their feet, Jesus honors the bodies of his disciples, grounding them in his own sacred vulnerability (John 13:1-20). A week after his resurrection, Jesus appears to the disciples with a spear scar in this side, nail scars in his hands, and presumably nail scars in his feet as well (John 20:27). Jesus' resurrected body is not blemish-free. His scarred feet remind us that Jesus suffered death for our sakes. Yet they also remind us that Jesus lived life for our sakes. That he walked the same paths we walk. And that his feet got dusty as he traveled from place to place, mostly on foot, to come and stand among us.

Standing on Common Ground

When Jesus calls disciples to follow him, he stands on the same ground, sits in the same boat, and walks on the same water (well, once) as they do. Jesus approaches them at eye level and addresses them in their native tongue. The message is embodied by the man, by this man who takes the time and makes the effort to stand with people in their joys and sorrows.

Nat, a friend of mine, goes to stand with people in their times of need. He doesn't get bogged down by details of how or why someone is in distress. When Nat hears that he's needed, he climbs into his old Saab and heads out, whether to the hospital, to the church, or to someone's home. It might sound presumptuous simply to show up this way. Perhaps Nat's guileless way comes from his experience as a surgeon who has stood beside vulnerable people for many years. But I suspect Nat goes to stand with others because, as a follower of Jesus, he has beautiful feet.

"How beautiful are the feet of those who bring good news!" says the apostle Paul (Rom. 10:15), quoting the prophet Isaiah (52:7). Paul recognizes that the best way to speak faithful words to others and share the love of Christ with them is to go and stand with them. When we literally share common ground with others, we share their humanity, and they share ours. It might not seem like the most efficient use of time and resources, but going to stand beside another conveys profound regard, care, and honor for that person. In this age of high-speed and widely available communication technology, the physical presence of a person standing beside you bears powerful witness to God's incarnate grace.

"Almost Heaven . . ."

On a mission trip to rural West Virginia, Ryan had looked forward to a week of construction work with fellow team members. Instead, his coleaders asked Ryan to help lead a Bible club for young children from the community. Ryan did not feel comfortable working with young children and didn't consider this one of his gifts. But as one of the adult leaders, he reluctantly stepped forward for this assignment.

"As the other fellas sported their work boots and carpenter pants and loaded power sanders and two-by-fours into their vans, I donned a pair of trail shorts and flip-flops and found the biggest box of crayons I could heft to load up my vehicle," Ryan recalls. The Bible club teachers began setting up for the children, with Ryan dreading the day that lay ahead of him.

As youngsters arrived, they were asked to find a buddy from the mission team. Every little boy gravitated to Ryan and became his buddy throughout the week. "Mine were the beautiful feet bearing the good news for them," Ryan realized. "They loved it—not because I knew funny songs to sing, not because I particularly knew how to relate to them (I didn't). They loved it just because I was there without pretense or agenda. I was just there for them. We cannot underestimate the ministry of presence."

Accompaniment

We go to stand with others; we walk beside them in faith. When we do, we become aware that Christ comes alongside to accompany us on the journey. Sound familiar? Indeed, the Emmaus Road story (Luke 24) offers an account of accompaniment that can shape how we view ourselves in mission partnership with others.

As you recall, two of Jesus' followers are walking the seven-mile road from Jerusalem to the village of Emmaus. As Cleopas and his unnamed companion walk and talk together, they are joined by Jesus, whom they don't recognize. This "stranger" asks them what they're discussing, and they're incredulous that he's the only one in town unaware of the crucifixion. Jesus opens the scriptures to them but doesn't yet disclose his identity. When the three arrive in Emmaus, the two followers urge Jesus to stay with them. When he breaks bread with them at table, their eyes are opened and they finally recognize him as the risen Lord. Cleopas and his companion then hightail it back to Jerusalem, braving the night darkness to share the good news with other disciples.

We serve others most profoundly not by giving them things or by doing things for them but by accompanying them on their way.

The Emmaus Road story teaches what *accompaniment* means: walking together, sharing in conversation about what really matters, extending hospitality to strangers, breaking bread together. Companions trust that Christ joins us on the journey, reveals God's love for us in Word and Table fellowship, and fills us with good courage to go forth in his name. We serve others most profoundly not by giving them things or by doing things for them but by accompanying them on their way. Our feet become "beautiful" as we walk together, because the One who accompanies us has the most beautiful feet of all.

Fishing for Followers

With respect to framing mission trips, "standing with others" and "walking with others" avoid the problematic image of "fishing for others." The fishing image comes from Gospel accounts in which Jesus calls disciples to follow him. In Matthew 4:18-22, Jesus walks by the Sea of Galilee and calls fishermen brothers Simon Peter and Andrew, then James and John, simply by saying, "Follow me, and I will make you fish for people." In Luke 5:1-11, Jesus gives Simon Peter a fishing lesson that results in a boat-sinking haul. He then tells the stunned fisherman, "Do not be afraid; from now on you will be catching people."

In both versions Jesus presents the call to discipleship in terms simple fishermen can readily grasp. Jesus' followers will still be "fishing" for a living, though in a figurative rather than literal sense. Right from the start, Jesus implies that following him means extending his ministry to others, to people who will be fished for and caught.

As mission-team members we're inspired by these Gospel fish tales because we identify ourselves with those disciples called to leave behind home and work commitments to follow Jesus. We're encouraged by Jesus' reassuring words, "Don't be afraid. You're on my team now. Together we can do this."

The fishing metaphor is not reassuring to people who are being fished for, however. Whether for food or sport, an angler catches a fish by luring it onto a disguised hook. Other fisher folk use spears or nets to snag their prey. The modern term *phishing* plays on the predatory nature of this activity. If you spend any time online, you know that phishing is the attempt to steal credit card or password information by masquerading as a trustworthy person or business. Anyone with an e-mail address can be lured into a trap by the deceptive graphics and official-sounding words of a phishing scam. Nobody likes to be "phished for" or "caught" in someone's net.

Catch and Release

A mission team is not deputized to fish for and catch people. Even when Jesus speaks of "catching people," he does so with an important twist. Luke's Gospel ties the miracle of the great catch to the theme of release announced in the preceding chapter: "[God] has sent me to proclaim release to the captives" (Luke 4:18). Simon Peter and his fishing partners were slaving away to benefit Rome, not their own families or community. Since occupation, Romans had developed quite a taste for salted fish harvested from the Sea of Galilee. By the time of Jesus' ministry, this big freshwater lake had been overfished. Thus the exclamation, "Master, we have worked all night long but have caught nothing." And thus the astonishment at the great catch, followed by grateful release from serving the empire.

We can use this fish tale with our mission team if we keep this catch-and-release theme in mind. We can *name the nets* in which we find ourselves caught and from which Jesus seeks to release us. We need to name them at the personal level, as Simon Peter did: "Go away from me, Lord, for I am a sinful man!" We also need to name the social and political nets in which we find ourselves entangled: In what ways does my daily work advance empire building? serve the interests of consumer culture? promote the powerful at the expense of the powerless? As I serve in mission, how is Jesus releasing me, setting me free to lay down these nets? How might "fishing for and catching people" for Jesus' sake extend the invitation to everyone to lay down nets that bind and enslave?

No fishing for answers or fishing for compliments allowed!

Dusty Feet Revisited

Luke 10 is another problematic passage when used to frame mission trips. Jesus deputizes seventy followers and sends them out in pairs to reconnoiter towns he plans to visit. Jesus instructs them to travel light, share peace with every household that welcomes them, and mind their manners. So far, so good. But then Jesus warns disciples that he is sending them out "like lambs into the midst of wolves," and he counsels them to handle rejection by shaking the dust off their feet as a protest. Who are these "wolves" to whom Jesus refers? And why is he convinced that certain households will not welcome his followers?

Luke writes during a period of mounting tension between Judeans and Samaritans. Judeans view Samaritans as apostate Jews, half-breeds who have sold their birthright through intermarriage to non-Jews during the Exile. Since they are not welcome to worship in the Jerusalem Temple, Samaritans worship God on Mount Gerizim. Samaritans obey only the law of Moses, meaning they don't sing the psalms, read the prophets, or respect the household of King David. Jesus was well aware of this sibling rivalry, as his disciples wanted to rain fire down on a Samaritan village that had been inhospitable to their ministry (Luke 9:51-56). So when Jesus talks about "wolves" and rude receptions, the disciples know just who he as in mind: those good-for-nothing Samaritans.

Jesus' story of the *good* Samaritan is set precisely in this climate of mutual mistrust (10:25-37). From the outset, those hearing Jesus' parable identify with the man who had been attacked. They see themselves as the man in the ditch and nod knowingly as both the priest and the Levite pass by on the other side. They expect the third person coming down the road to be a righteous Judean, one of their own. But what if the dusty feet that come to your aid belong to your archenemy? What if the calloused hands that reach out to help you have prayed to a different god? Will you swallow your pride and accept assistance from this "neighbor"? Can you bring yourself to trust this "wolf" with your well-being? with your very life?

Jesus' Judean hearers are shocked when the story's hero turns out to be a hated Samaritan. And any self-respecting Samaritan would be offended at the mere thought of giving such attentive care to a Judean. No one finds the scandalous outcome of this story pleasing!

And yet . . . the story must have clicked for someone, because it made its way into Luke's Gospel and later into the Acts of the Apostles, in which Luke proclaims the successful spread of the gospel through Samaria (Acts 8). The parable of the good Samaritan has fired the imagination of Christians throughout the centuries. The lawyer's question to Jesus still rings in our ears today: "Who is my neighbor?" (Luke 10:29). Sometimes it is the very person we had considered "a wolf."

Peaceable Kingdom

A mission trip undertaken by Francis of Assisi changed his understanding about Jesus sending "lambs into the midst of wolves." In 1219 Francis and a few companions left on a pilgrimage of nonviolence to Egypt. A Crusade was underway, and Francis felt that convincing the Muslim leader to convert to Christianity could prevent hostilities. Francis boldly and foolishly (as in "a fool for Christ") crossed the enemy line and was received graciously by the sultan.

Barefoot and clad in a coarse garment—Francis's attire since his own conversion and in the spirit of Matthew 10:9—Francis preached the gospel. The sultan was not swayed to accept Christ. However, the two men gained great respect for each other during their conversations over a couple of weeks. And Francis was inspired by Isaiah's vision of the peaceable kingdom, especially the verse prophesying that "the wolf shall live with the lamb" (Isa.11:6). Perhaps Christians, Muslims, and Jews could learn to coexist without killing one another? Each group currently considered itself "a lamb" surrounded by "wolves." Perhaps living in mutual respect would realize Isaiah's vision?

Francis proposed an armistice between Christian and Muslim forces. He drew up the terms of the treaty, to which the sultan agreed. The Crusade leaders, itching for battle, rejected the agreement and condemned Francis as a heretic, punishable by death. They refused to see the beautiful, bare feet of this messenger who announced peace and brought good news (Isa. 52:7). The sultan did regard Francis's feet and helped him to escape and return to Italy. Warfare ensued and continues to this day.

Legend has it that Francis once tamed a ferocious wolf that was terrorizing the Italian town of Gubbio, devouring people as well as animals. Francis went into the hills to find the predator. He made the sign of the cross and commanded "Brother Wolf" to hurt no one. The wolf closed its jaws and lay down at Francis' beautiful, bare feet. Then Francis led the wolf into town to make peace with the startled citizens. They agreed to feed the wolf regularly, and the wolf agreed no longer to prey on them or their flocks.

The legend of Francis and the wolf and the story of Francis and the sultan give us glimpses of the peaceable kingdom drawing near, even as predation and violence persist in this world. Just as he called Francis, Jesus calls disciples in every age to stride forth with confidence as humble ambassadors of peace. As we stand on common ground with others—creatures as well as humans—we find ourselves standing together on holy ground. The ground is made holy because another has come to stand with us and walk beside us. We don't always recognize his face, but we can tell who he is by his beautiful, scarred feet.

For the Journey

Before the trip, trace outlines of each team member's bare foot on construction paper. Write the person's name on each foot. Create a mission-trip display featuring these feet and the caption "How beautiful are the feet of those who bring good news."

Before the trip, ask team members to reflect on this question: How will we tread lightly on our trip, careful not to leave huge footprints where we walk? For example, North Americans are becoming aware of our collective "carbon footprint"—the total amount of CO_2 and other greenhouse gases emitted over the full life cycle of a product or service. What steps can we take to reduce the size of that footprint, especially as it affects the Two-Thirds World? One congregation commits to a "carbon fast" during Lent. Members do something every day to limit the amount of carbon dioxide emissions they produce.

God said to Moses, "Remove the sandals from your feet, for the place on which you are standing is holy ground" (Exod. 3:5). While on the road, read the Exodus passage and invite team members to ponder: What "shoes" are protecting me from touching holy ground in this place? Am I willing to remove those shoes?

During the trip, pay attention to the feet of people you meet. What, if anything, do they wear to protect their feet? Where do they get their footwear, and at what price? Are shoes repairable or do they tend to be disposable?

Learn more about Saint Francis of Assisi. Each day of your trip, share a different story about his life and ministry with your group.

Plan a foot-washing service for team members after a day of hard, dusty work. Use a water pitcher, a basin, and plenty of clean towels.

Lord, you have been our dwelling place in all generations.

Before the mountains were brought forth,

or ever you had formed the earth and the world,

from everlasting to everlasting you are God.

. . . .

Let your work be manifest to your servants,

and your glorious power to their children.

Let the favor of the Lord our God be upon us,

and prosper for us the work of our hands—

O prosper the work of our hands!—Psalm 90:1-2, 16-17

Gracious God,

Open our eyes to your work unfolding among us.

Open our ears to hear your voice calling us.

Open our arms to the needy ones around us.

Gladden our hearts with the joy of serving others

and the delight of pleasing you.

Bless the work we do.

Amen.

—Susan Briehl

7
Open Hands

One January I led a half dozen seminary students on a service-learning trip to Puerto Rico. While we worked in the interior mountains, heavy rains caused severe flooding throughout the coastal areas. Several days later, we drove down to San Juan only to discover that a scheduled activity had to be cancelled due to the flooding. Initially we were tempted to find something else for our group to *do*. With just three days left for our stay on the island, it only made sense to "seize the day."

But then one wise student observed, "You know, we've been going nonstop for a full week. Even Sunday was filled with worship and fellowship activities. What if we just took a day off?"

"Yeah," another student jumped in. "It's like that story about the monk sitting beside the road. Someone stops to offer help and he says, 'No thanks. I've been traveling this road for several days, and I'm just waiting for my soul to catch up with my body.' I sort of feel that way about now."

"Can we do this?" the students asked, looking in my direction. "Can we justify taking a day off?" As trip leader, I was responsible for approving any curriculum changes.

"Well," I replied, struggling to suppress my productivity genes. "Today is Wednesday, but I guess there's no law against proclaiming

Wednesday a day of rest. I could honestly use a nap myself. Let's gather after dinner to share what we've learned from our midweek break." Always the teacher!

We did gather that evening to share stories of our day. One student had found candles in the kitchen cabinet, and our faces were now bathed in warm candlelight. Another passed around a plate of delicious pastries from a local market. Several of us showed the sand flea bites we got from swimming in the sea. A student read a poem about a child she met while walking on the beach. Everyone seemed refreshed, restored, renewed. Like those quietly burning candles, our spirits were light and at peace.

"I really enjoy being together with you guys," began one student, grinning sheepishly. "But it was sure great not being cooped up all day in the van with you!" After we laughed and nodded in agreement, he continued, "I've been thinking about that van, though, and wondering how we might use it to help some of the recent flood victims. Perhaps we could transport supplies as part of the relief effort?"

"Yes!" another student chimed in. "I read in today's paper that the main road is now open, and supply trucks are on the move. We could load up donated clothes and first aid supplies and head down there tomorrow."

"We're supposed to meet with a local pastor tomorrow," added a third student. "So maybe he can ride along with us, and we'll have our meeting on the van. I think he'd be game, if we can figure a way to help those folks."

As we sat with this emerging plan, it occurred to us that this idea had come as a gift. It's not something we would have imagined or embraced had we remained on-task and agenda-driven. We first had to release our grip on the planned schedule and let go of our control needs for a day. When we did that, a gift was placed in our open, receptive hands; we discerned a calling to serve and found ourselves Spirit-led down a path we had not anticipated traveling together.

The Gift of Sabbath

The gift placed in our open hands was the gift of sabbath. God gave the Israelites *shabbat*—the gift of sabbath—when they were freed from slavery in Egypt. The gift was expressed as a command: "Observe the sabbath day and keep it holy. . . . Six days you shall labor and do all your work. But the seventh day is a sabbath to the LORD your God; you shall not do any work" (Deut. 5:12-14).

What a radical concept! God knew that if those freed slaves didn't keep the sabbath, they would soon enslave themselves to ceaseless commerce. God gave the fourth commandment to subvert business as usual, to help us say no to the endless cycle of producing and consuming that threatens to suck the life right out of us. God also gave this commandment to foster re-creation and delight, feasting with family and friends, and embracing life-giving activities. Sabbath creates space to discern new callings and allows open hands to take up new initiatives.

Having enjoyed sabbath rest, our seminary crew procured donations and made the trip to a flood-ravaged village the following day. The local pastor eagerly came with us; he knew people affected by the flood and had no vehicle to drive there himself. He was just the guide we needed and inspired us with stories about his life and ministry.

We spent the better part of a day packed like sardines in that van, yet no one seemed to mind. Because we had been blessed by sabbath freedom from one another, we were now set free for one another and for strangers whom we felt called to serve. It will come as no surprise that students rated this sabbath-and-service experience the most valuable learning from that trip.

Keeping sabbath is one of the most challenging spiritual disciplines for mission-trip leaders. We realize how precious our time is on the road. We don't want to disappoint people who have carved valuable days out of their schedule to serve. We want to be faithful stewards of the funds raised to support this mission. There's much to do and so little time to do it! How can we afford to lay down our tools, suspend activities, and kick back for a day?

Gospel Wisdom

Jesus' disciples also felt a sense of urgency when they were sent out in his name to preach and teach and heal. The Gospel of Mark says, "Many were coming and going, and they had no leisure even to eat." So Jesus tells them, "Come away to a deserted place all by yourselves and rest a while" (6:31).

Now you can almost hear Peter and the others protest, "But Master, the people's need is so great, and you've given us the power to help them. This is no time for a vacation! We need to keep moving, full steam ahead." Yet Jesus persists, and it is in this context that Jesus feeds not only his disciples but five thousand others who were following after them. He feeds the multitude by blessing and breaking five loaves and two fish.

Worldly wisdom says, "Keep going 24/7. Seize the day. Don't stop 'til you drop." But gospel wisdom honors the body, respects our needs as finite creatures for rest and renewal. Gospel wisdom trusts that receiving the day with open hands creates space for God's providence to unfold. What unfolds, we discover, may far surpass our own schemes and imaginings. Gospel wisdom commands us to keep the sabbath. Instead of going 24/7, we observe a day to cease from labor, to give others a day off as well.

If you're familiar with the restaurant chain Chick-fil-A, you know their stores are closed on Sundays. Worldly wisdom said, "A fast-food restaurant has to stay open on Sunday—that's a prime business day." But founder Truett Cathy said, "Our decision to close on Sunday was our way of honoring God and of directing our attention to things that mattered more than our business." Cathy believed that all employees deserve a full day of rest with their families. He was convinced this would yield healthier, more productive workers. And he trusted that customers would respect these values and patronize Chick-fil-A the other six days of the week.

Well, guess what? Cathy's foolish wisdom proved to be right. Chick-fil-A has a loyal customer base, including my daughter! The company's stand-alone restaurants achieve higher sales in six days than other fast-food restaurants do in seven. And Chick-fil-A enjoys the highest employee satisfaction and lowest turnover in the entire industry.

Worldly wisdom promises that efficiency will free us from the constraints of time. But worldly wisdom actually enslaves us to the clock all the more. Gospel wisdom frees us precisely by centering us in God's gift of time, by offering us sabbath rest, by encouraging us to receive each day as a gift instead of a burden.

Lord of the Sabbath

Jesus extended the meaning of sabbath in regard to two life-giving initiatives: open eating and open healing. The religious authorities kept a vigilant eye on what, when, and with whom people ate. They monitored the purity laws, determining who was "clean" and who was "unclean." People in need of healing were often consigned to the "unclean" list until the priests pronounced them "clean/whole/healed." Eating and healing mattered to these religious leaders not because they were nitpicky but because they were trying so hard to preserve Jewish identity in the face of relentless Roman oppression.

Early in his ministry Jesus proclaimed God's merciful reign as an open, bountiful table to which all are invited. When his hungry disciples plucked grain to eat on the sabbath, Jesus reminded peeved Pharisees that meeting basic human need constituted lawful sabbath activity. "The sabbath was made for humankind, and not humankind for the sabbath," Jesus exclaimed. "So the Son of Man is lord even of the sabbath" (Mark 2:27-28).

Also on the sabbath, Jesus showed that God's healing power is available to all, not just to those favored by priestly authorities. Right under their noses, Jesus healed a man with a withered hand. "Stretch out your hand," Jesus said to the man. "He stretched it out, and his hand was restored" (Mark 3:5). Restored to pick up tools and work during six days of the week; to give and receive affection; to break bread with family and friends. And restored also to refrain from commerce, to lift up prayers, to keep the sabbath—which Jesus was ironically accused of violating.

As followers of Jesus, we know that keeping sabbath is about more than just taking a day off. It is about stretching out our hands in faith, trusting God to heal and restore, to give us our daily bread, to set us free from whatever enslaves us. On mission trips sabbath releases us from the tyranny of our many scheduled activities so that we might pay attention to God's surprising activity in the world. With open hands we are ready to receive gifts even from those we have come to serve.

Open Hands, Open Hearts

Jesus sends out disciples two-by-two with little in their hands— only a staff according to Mark 6, and no staff according to Matthew 10 and Luke 9. No bag, no bread, no extra tunic. Jesus instructs them to travel with open, empty hands rather than hands filled with stuff. He does not advise them to take toys and trinkets for the kids they'll meet along the way. They don't even pack hostess gifts for the kind folks who will offer them food and shelter as they travel from village to village. Seems rather inconsiderate, don't you think? What does Jesus have in mind sending out his disciples so unprepared?

Perhaps Jesus views preparation in a different light. Recalling his own temptation in the wilderness, Jesus knows how easily we human beings can be swayed to put our trust in worldly things—even necessities such as food and religion—rather than in God. Going forth empty-handed prepares the disciples to trust in God's providence rather than in their own resourcefulness. The disciples' openhanded posture also prepares their hosts to receive them "just as they are," without expecting compensation or reward. This keeps the focus on the message, the good news Jesus' disciples have come to proclaim.

On mission trips we often find ourselves serving others who have far less stuff than we have. It feels inconsiderate arriving empty-handed, when we have so much we could give away without even missing it. Yet we go to be among others with open, receptive hands, not with cargo-laden hands. It might make us feel good to shower people with handouts, but this is not a time to play Santa Claus. Gifts must be given with great care and forethought so as not to be disruptive for a community or create a dependency relationship that will be unhealthy for future mission teams.

Whatever we carry as we go forth in mission, let us hold it lightly, with open hands.

Close consultation with the host community leads to appropriate gift giving. With approval from community members, a mission team could bring books for a local school or library. Clothing and sewing materials could be donated to a church clothes closet. Small toy prizes could be collected to use as incentives for children attending a dental clinic. Such gifts would benefit the entire community and not incite jealousy between those who receive gifts and those who don't.

Whatever we carry as we go forth in mission, let us hold it lightly, with open hands. As we let go, in trust and humility, of our cargo and our calendars and our control needs, we open our hearts to God's amazing grace that will sustain us each day, and for our whole lives.

For the Journey

Identify obstacles that currently prevent you from keeping sabbath: pressures to work, the lure of the market, organized sports, spending time online, or other influences. Read Deuteronomy 5:12-15. To what things will you need to say no in order to say yes to sabbath rest and renewal?

Before your trip, invite mission-team members to try one of the following disciplines on a given Sunday and report back to the group how this affected their day:

- Don't buy anything.
- Walk or ride a bike instead of driving the car.
- Go the whole day without wearing a watch.
- Prepare and enjoy Sunday dinner with another family.
- Take a nature hike and carry a bag to pick up any litter you come across.
- Bring pillows to church and take an hour-long group nap.

What do you notice about how you relate to time while on the road? Do you feel more free or more constrained? What about the people with whom you serve—how do they relate to time? Do they have the same sense of punctuality as your team? If not, how does this affect shared activities? What strategies will help your team cope when chronological sensibilities clash (for example, when waiting at a work site for supplies scheduled to be delivered before you arrived)? If traveling south of the border, did your group take a siesta? What was that like for you?

The fourth commandment calls for rest for all creatures, not just for people in power who can afford it. This includes travelers, hired hands, animals, and even the earth itself. How can time-privileged individuals be advocates for those who are not?

Invite your leadership team to read *Receiving the Day: A Guide for Conversation*, by Dorothy Bass, and the "Time" chapter in *Way to Live*. A study guide for Receiving the Day is available in the online library of www.practicingourfaith.org.

[God] opened the rock, and water gushed out;

it flowed through the desert like a river.—*Psalm 105:41*

God of wonderful works,
glory be to your name.

When your children were slaves,
you set them free.
When your children were thirsty,
you cracked open the rock in the desert.
When your children were hungry,
you sent quails from the sky
and bread from the heavens.
And when your children came to the land of milk
and honey,
you made it home.

God of the promised land,
glory be to your name.
Come, make a home with your children.

—*J. Bradley Wigger*

8

Courageous Lips

It began as an innocent request, a simple accommodation. Our North Carolina church mission team of fifteen teens and adults was serving with our partner church in Coatepeque, Guatemala. Members of La Iglesia Jerusalém (Jerusalem Presbyterian Church) knocked themselves out anticipating our needs and offering heart-felt hospitality. Every morning, for instance, they served us a deli-cious breakfast with fresh-squeezed orange juice . . . until Rebecca asked if she could have a Diet Coke for breakfast.

The next morning, a can of Diet Coke sat beside everyone's breakfast plate. Not a glass of OJ in sight. I missed my glass of fresh-squeezed juice! And I cringed realizing our Guatemalan hosts must be thinking that we Americans drink Coke with every meal. But I didn't give Rebecca too much grief. We're in a country where it's safer to drink a canned or bottled beverage than something set before you in a glass.

Don't Drink the Water

In Guatemala, as in many parts in the world, a water bottle becomes one's constant and necessary companion. Wherever our mission team went, we kept an eye out for the nearest bottle of *agua pura* to refill our personal water bottles. "Don't drink the water," we were warned, because in Guatemala, 98 percent of the water sources are contaminated. The country has few municipal water treatment systems, and even the treated water is unsafe to drink. We reminded one another to use bottled water for brushing teeth, and to close eyes and mouth while bathing. The locals take precautions as well. Their bodies are not resistant to the harmful bacteria swimming blithely in their city water supply.

We're creatures of habit, of course, so one of our North Carolina group would inevitably forget and rinse a toothbrush or mouth with tap water. It was like Lucy being kissed by Snoopy: "Oh my gosh!! Where's the Listerine bottle?!?" These incidents reminded our group that most of us who live in the U.S.A. take clean water for granted. For my part, I grew up near the Tennessee River. Every faucet in my suburban community dispensed clean running water, and I assumed that was true in most places. I never heard the word *potable* until I traveled abroad as a college student.

This is what I now know: though the world is awash in water, only 1 percent is fit for human consumption. Agriculture and industry consume most of that supply. So 40 percent of the world's population has no access to safe drinking water. Most disease in the Two-Thirds World results from contaminated water, and each year more than five million people—mostly children—die from waterborne diseases.

My mission-trip water bottle may be a temporary inconvenience for me. For millions of people it's a necessary way of life. They don't buy bottled water as a matter of taste preference, as we do. When they're able, they buy it so they won't get sick drinking from their own wells. In some countries, governments have sold local water rights to transnational corporations, meaning locals no longer have access to their own village wells. People walk long distances toting water for their families.

I want my water bottle to remind me of these realities. When I'm back in the States, mindlessly using gallons of fresh water for myself every day, I want to be jarred back into awareness that the rest of the world treats water as a precious resource. I want to learn how

I can be a better steward of water and how I can assist others in gaining access to clean water. When I hear the story of a tired, thirsty Jesus requesting a drink from the Samaritan woman at the well (John 4), I want to recall the tired, thirsty faces I've seen. "I was thirsty," Jesus will say on the day of great judgment, "and you gave me something to drink" (Matt. 25:35).

Thought for Food

Of the many ways we take in a travel experience, the most basic way we do so is through our mouths and digestive systems. Since we must daily nourish our bodies while on the road, we constantly confront choices about what in the world to eat. We may see plenty of potential food, but what's *safe* to eat? What can we ingest that won't make us sick? That's always a concern, of course, though a heightened concern when dining in unfamiliar places.

Travel puts our bodies at risk, renders us vulnerable to invisible microbes lurking in that tasty stew or unassuming cup of juice. Before going to Guatemala, our group memorized the mantra "Boil it, cook it, peel it, or forget it." We became hypervigilant about our diet, constantly checking in with each other, "Does this look okay to you? Do you think this is safe to eat?" No one was coerced into eating or drinking something that seemed unsafe, and our hosts understood our caution. Thankfully, most of us stayed healthy throughout most of the trip. Cipro, an antibiotic, came in handy when stomachs were compromised.

A mission team could consider food safety just a matter of convenience or logistics. We can plan our itinerary and meal schedule around the availability of the Golden Arches. Or we can become mindful of how our bodies are sustained by food—including fast food—while en route. Sharing meals can become an occasion for hospitality, for entrusting ourselves to hosts who relate to food differently than we do. We can talk openly about ways to be gracious when the food offered to us seems strange or unsafe to consume.

The Bible brims with food stories and images, so we can ponder how our own travel stories are joined to the biblical story. And we can gain perspective on our daily eating habits back home, reflecting on what we typically eat and drink, where our food is produced and at what cost, who in our community has access to food and who doesn't. We can view food sharing as a basic human activity that connects the dots of all these experiences across multiple contexts.

You Are What You Eat

"You are what you eat." My parents used to say that when I was a child, wishing I could have a candy bar instead of broccoli for supper. Parents throughout history have been dishing out this proverb to their kids, I suppose. Eating is, after all, a basic human activity. We can't photosynthesize like plants and create life practically out of thin air. We have to replenish our energy by ingesting carbon molecules stored up by plants or by plant eaters. As these molecules get reassembled in our body, what we eat actually becomes part of who we are.

As an adult I've grown fond of broccoli . . . and spinach . . . and all manner of vegetables. I also eat meat, though I prefer fish. On most days I crave salad more than meat, the exception being when I visit my hometown and feast on Gibson's Bar-B-Q. But one night before crossing the border to Mexico, my travel companions and I ate big dinner salads because we knew this would be the last safe salad we could eat for ten days. Tijuana is the birthplace of Caesar salad—what a shame that we wouldn't be able to eat one there! Leafy greens such as lettuce are simply unsafe to eat, and even a vegetable wash may not remove all harmful bacteria. Better safe than sorry.

Maintaining a healthy diet during a mission trip is challenging, especially for vegetarians. In many cultures hosts serve costly meat dishes as an expression of their generosity and honor for the guest. Recall the prodigal son's return home after his mischief: the joyful father orders his servants to kill the fatted calf—not dig up the ripe radishes—for a feast. As people in developing countries become more affluent, they eat fewer fruits and vegetables and more meat and processed foods. And like many North Americans, they soon become overweight.

Today, for the first time in human history, more people in the world are overfed than underfed. Millions still starve, of course, because of political upheavals (wars, for example) and inequitable distribution. People do not go hungry due to an inadequate world food supply, however. The world currently has a food *surplus*.

This global food glut now drives the aggressive advertising of food in every corner of the world. A typical supermarket in this country carries thirty to forty *thousand* items clambering over one another to get your attention: "Choose me, I taste better!" "Choose me, I'm healthier!" "Choose me, I've got the coolest packaging!" Meanwhile the produce section sits there quietly, minding its own business.

Jewish and Muslim traditions guide their members in what to eat, when to eat, and how to eat. Among Christian traditions, Seventh Day Adventists recommend a vegetarian, alcohol-free diet. But most Christians are left to fend for ourselves in figuring out what's for dinner. So advertisers have a field day pushing their food products on us. They also urge us to "eat global," so we now eat foods that travel an average of *fifteen hundred miles* to reach our plates, which consumes a lot of fossil fuel. And though we don't realize it, the way we eat in this country jeopardizes the food economies of other countries, especially our neighbors to the south.

Think Global, Eat Local

Here's an example of how our national food policies affect others. "We the people" subsidize U.S. farmers to grow massive amounts of cheap corn. Corn is the perfect industrial commodity because it can be broken down and reassembled in so many different ways. Turn four cents' worth of corn into high-fructose corn syrup, add a liter of water and some fizz, and you can sell it for a dollar. Some form of corn is now added to almost everything we eat. In a Chicken McNugget, thirteen out of thirty-eight ingredients derive from corn, including the corn-fed chicken itself. And most U.S. cattle now eat corn although their stomachs are designed to digest grass; this diet causes big-time stomachaches, which require massive doses of antibiotics.

Free-trade agreements (the North American Free Trade Agreement—NAFTA) allow our country to export tons of cheap corn to Mexico. As a result, the corn farmer in Chiapas gets shut out, and farmland that fed local folk for centuries now lies fallow. Throughout the global south, people are aggrieved that U.S. food policies undermine their own food security. When mission teams travel to these places, attentive eyes can notice what's happening. Are people able to eat local foods and live off the land? Or do they rely more on imported, processed foods? Have children been seduced by the allure of junk food? Are they drinking Diet Coke instead of fresh-squeezed orange juice for breakfast?

Perhaps we would eat less meat, and with more reverence, if we saw the actual animals that become our food.

✦

A U.S. mission team in the Yucatán noticed a tethered cow grazing in the small yard of a nearby market. They figured the cow was someone's pet and greeted "Bessie" each day as they passed by on the way to their work site. On the final morning of their stay, mission-team members were shocked to see half the village lined up outside the market, waiting to buy a slice of "Bessie." As one team member commented, "It all seemed so in-your-face and personal, so different from how we buy shrink-wrapped cuts of meat in the grocery store."

Indeed, eating "food with a face" is a humbling experience, connecting us with the particular creature who gave its life (not willingly!) to nourish human life. Perhaps we would eat less meat, and with more reverence, if we saw the actual animals that become our food. What would greater transparency mean in planning the menu for our daily meals? What would it mean to the meatpacking industry, whose workers come increasingly from south of the border? And what would it mean for the animals themselves to live according to their creaturely nature instead of being reduced to mere "production units"?

Daily Bread

The Bible has wisdom to offer in shaping our food practices. Consider the story of those hungry Israelites wandering in the wilderness, nourished by God's provision of a strange white substance that caused the people to wonder "*Manna?*" (Hebrew for "What is it?"—see Exod. 16:15). This is a fitting story to recall when we're on the road and the provisions seem scarce, or the food served looks unappetizing. How might the memory of manna give us courageous and grateful lips instead of complaining ones? In what ways does God's mercy sustain us with the "daily bread" we need for survival?

When the Hebrew people had settled in Israel and Judah, they recalled God's provision of daily bread through supporting the practice of gleaning. Instead of harvesting a field completely, reapers would leave grain behind for poor people and sojourners to gather. The story of Ruth, great-grandmother of King David, unfolds in the barley fields where this Moabite woman gleans grain under the watchful eye of Boaz, the landowner who soon becomes her husband.

Today the biblical practice of gleaning inspires ministries such as the Society of Saint Andrew (www.endhunger.org). Through initiatives such as the Potato Project, the Gleaning Network, and Harvest of Hope, volunteers participate in hand-harvesting and redistributing produce to hungry people. Gleaning can be a compelling outreach ministry for mission teams that wish to focus explicitly on hunger relief.

Gospel Gumbo

The Gospels portray an earthly messiah who cares about food. According to John, Jesus performs his first sign, or miracle, by changing water into wine at a wedding feast in Cana of Galilee. A mission team could ponder the "water into wine" image, reflecting on where they have experienced such transformation during their service. Jesus doesn't change wine into water but water into wine, a radical change that improves quality. This change makes life fuller, more joyful, more fragrant, more colorful. With Jesus, there is always more, and the best is yet to come. And as the gospel pours forth to fill every emptiness in the world, we can count on Jesus to change things—not just for people but for all creation. A wise poet once observed about this miracle, "The modest water beheld its Lord, and blushed."

Throughout his earthly ministry, Jesus promotes a radical open eating program that upsets religious authorities. The authorities especially object to Jesus' choice of dinner companions, those with whom he breaks bread. To share food with others is to share humanity with them, to share openly our contingency and need. How dare Rabbi Jesus open himself to all manner of people in this way? Has he no self-respect, no sense of propriety or discretion? How humiliating to watch an emerging Jewish leader be so indiscriminate, so casual and careless with regard to purity codes. Eating with "the wrong crowd" undermines Jewish faith, already threatened by Roman occupation. Consider Jesus' encounter with Zacchaeus in Luke 19:1-10 as retold by John Shea:

> Even when Jesus was a guest
> he slipped into being a host.
> Once on his way through Jericho
> a dwarf of a tax collector, Zacchaeus by name,
> whose eyes were as tarnished as Roman coins
> and whose hands were no bigger than a stolen purse
> climbed a tree to spot Jesus.
> But Jesus spied him.
> "Zacchaeus, hurry down.
> Tonight I dine at your house."
> Now who is host and who is guest
> when one invites and one accepts?
> What can happen at a meal?

Can more than bread be shared?
Can more than wine be drunk?
In the morning Zacchaeus pulled the rusted key
from the center of his soul
and opened the locked boxes
where he kept the sweat of his country.
The people came and reclaimed
from the tall Zacchaeus
what the small man had taken.

Just as he did at the wedding feast in Cana, Jesus switches from guest to host by inviting himself to Zacchaeus's house, then offering hospitality to one who was despised because of his collaboration with Roman oppressors. Mission and service teams often experience role reversals. Think and talk about any experiences like this your group has had or might anticipate.

Extending the Table

The first Christians gathered around a table to remember Jesus' last supper, his death, and his resurrection. The early church began as a meal fellowship. Wherever house churches sprang up, dining rooms were literally expanded to hold larger tables to feed the faithful and especially the poor. The table was extended figuratively as well. At Paul's prodding, Gentiles as well as Jews were included in Christian meal fellowship.

Let the Lord's Table shape the way your mission team eats throughout your trip. First, share a eucharistic meal with the community you are serving. For some groups, this may need to take the form of an agape love feast rather than ritual Communion. However observed, find ways to connect to local meal practices, perhaps with local staple food and festive drink. "Each culture has its own unique form of bread—baguette, challah, tortilla, naan," notes theologian David Hadley Jensen. "The risen Christ, accordingly, does not come in a meal that is specific to one culture alone." Fill the cup with wine, grape juice, or a fitting festival beverage that is both bitter and sweet.

Second, let the Lord's Table commend the enjoyment of food at every table. While on the road, plan for sit-down meals that are more than fast-food refueling. Take turns leading table blessings, and reflect on the day's activities. While on location, resist the urge to rush through meals in order to get to your work sites. Tarry at the table, especially when breaking bread with gracious hosts who have prepared and served the food. With your hosts, plan at least one feast or fiesta with music, decorations, and abundant food. Feasting celebrates abundance, even when the meal itself is meager. In our central Christian meal, even a morsel of bread and a sip of wine become a feast. Every sabbath is a fitting day for a feast.

Third, consider occasions when your mission team might fast or abstain from food. This challenge goes right to the gut! That's why the desert monastic Evagrius of Pontus listed *gluttony* as the first of the "eight deadly thoughts" (later revised by Gregory the Great as the "seven deadly sins"). Writing in the fourth century, Evagrius realized that legitimate concern for one's health can lead to eating too much or eating at the wrong time. Controlling one's appetite, he urged, would result in having more food to share, especially with the urban unemployed and with widows and orphans. Relinquishing one's obsession with food makes room for communion with God.

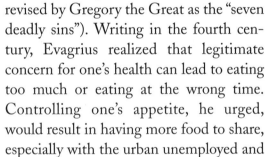

Relinquishing one's obsession with food makes room for communion with God.

Travel can jar awareness of appetite, especially for those accustomed to having food at their fingertips. Grazing throughout the day is not always an option. Snacks may not be available to quell every hunger pang. Rather than deplore the lack of convenience food, the wise leader can create a learning opportunity for the mission team. Commend *fasting* as a spiritual discipline. Fasting can bind us in solidarity with people whose hunger is constant. Cassian, a contemporary of Evagrius, advocated fasting between meals by not snacking whenever we feel that twinge of hunger. Invite team members to avoid munching on junk food during a leg of your journey. During your next meal, ask those who fasted to share how abstaining from "mindless eating" can make one a more mindful, thankful eater.

Mission trips offer an opportunity to cultivate mindful eating, to focus on food sharing in a more intentional way than many of us do in our daily lives. North Americans typically engage in "random acts of nutrition" rather than sit-down meals with our respective households. Even when we do eat dinner on the same schedule with our family, we're apt to roam around the kitchen waiting to heat our own personal meals in the microwave. At the dining room table we may cross paths with other family members for a few minutes each day. Hardly a robust table life, a way of eating that nourishes both body and soul.

Sharing life together on the road can remind us that it doesn't have to be this way. Throughout our lives, God gives us companions—literally "those with whom to eat bread." Jesus begins his public ministry by gathering a group of travel companions to share food and life together. These disciples so closely associate Jesus with companionship that to this day, Jesus' followers continue the meal fellowship he inaugurated. Nourished by fragments of bread and sips from a cup, courageous lips proclaim that Jesus is our constant companion still and welcomes everyone to join him at this meal.

If we are what we eat, then we are most profoundly what we eat and drink at Jesus' Table of grace. More than corn or organic food or anything else we may eat, this feast sustains us for faithful life in this world as well as life in the world to come.

For the Journey

Before your mission trip, your group might study the curriculum titled *Just Eating? Practicing Our Faith at the Table*. It calls Christians to reflect on four aspects of our lives with food:

- the health of our bodies

- the access others have to food

- the health of the earth, which our food choices influence

- the ways we use food to extend hospitality and enrich relationships.

Tour a supermarket and observe how food items are displayed. Marion Nestle notes that supermarkets are no longer in the business of selling food but make their money by selling real estate. Supermarkets sell the prime shelf space to the highest bidder, ensuring that this product gets eye-level placement as you stroll down the aisle. High-profit foods are placed at the end of the aisle or by the cash register to encourage the impulse purchase. Check this out when you're in the store. Where are the healthy cereals? Way up high or down low? Where are the sugar-loaded cereals? Right at eye level—for the children who nag their parents to death until a box of Captain Crunch lands in the cart. In some studies market researchers concluded that the impact of "the nag factor" (aka "pester power") contributes to almost half the sales of a target product. Nestle advises mindful eaters to avoid the center aisles and avoid items that have long ingredient lists.

Before the trip, discuss what foods you will most miss while on the road. During travels, share stories of how food plays a role in hospitality given and received. Recall a special meal and what made it memorable for you. What foods were shared? What blessings offered? After the trip, identify ways you have become more mindful eaters.

Practice expressing gratitude to hosts, even for food you deem unsafe to eat. How can you receive what is offered with a thankful heart but not feel obligated to eat or drink if you believe it could make you sick?

Prepare a loaf of the bread you use at home for a Communion service on the road. Take note of the type of bread used for Communion where you serve in mission.

Explore the differences between a fast-food meal and a Communion meal. Gather the group around a table and place a Big Mac meal alongside Communion elements. Invite learners to identify assumptions informing each meal. Provide categories for comparison: portion size, number of servings per meal, packaging, production costs (including carbon footprint), consumer price, standardized or varied according to host culture. Share insights as a plenary group and discuss implications for eating each meal.

Take steps toward ethical eating:

- Oppose the inhumane treatment of domestic animals in our care.
- Partner with local food producers (see www.localharvest.org and www.locavores.com).
- Reflect on biblical stories and images that involve food.
- Recover our enjoyment of food as God's good gift.
- Relate the Eucharistic Table to daily table life (see "Food" chapter in *Way to Live*).

Before a trip: Ask team members to research global water statistics. Learn what you can about the water supply where you'll be working. The world is awash in water. But 97 percent is salty, and 2 percent is frozen, leaving only 1 percent of all water fit for human consumption. Of that supply, 70 percent is used for agriculture and 20 percent for industry, leaving only 10 percent for households worldwide. Some places have abundant fresh water, while others don't. Forty percent of the world's population has no access to safe drinking water. Most disease in the Two-Thirds World is caused by unsafe water, and each year more than 5 million people—mostly children—die from water-related diseases.

During a trip, ask: Where can strategic intervention provide water purification for our hosts? Who would be responsible for maintaining the system if installed? Reflect together on Gospel passages in which Jesus offers "living water" (John 4) and advises followers how to be sheep instead of goats: "I was thirsty, and you gave me something to drink" (Matt. 25:35).

Thanks for the dank earth, awakened by vernal warmth,
shooting skyward skunky onion and asparagus spears,
volatizing viburnum and unwrapping wisteria blossom,
welcoming the staggering newborn lamb's steaming wool.

Praise for lengthy days, blades of new-mown grass
and honeysuckle hanging heavy in humid dusk,
homegrown tomato slices glistening like dew,
and barbeque smoking on the grill.

Glory in leaves that show their true colors,
surrender en masse,
then perfume the air with their slow decay, taunting
thirsty yellow jackets drawn to dirt-smeared sweatshirts,
crushed cranberries, nutmeg-rich pumpkin pie.

Delight in wondrous wet snow,
springing loose the fir and hemlock scent,
inviting candle lighting, chowder, and hot spiced cider.
Yule logs crackle and embers dance on the hearth;
We burrow beneath Grandma's patchwork quilt for warmth.

In every season,
our prayers rise as incense before you, O God;
our mouths melt morsels of yeasty wheat,
our tongues taste tangy fruit,
full-bodied and full-orbed,
for our salvation and for the sake of the world.

—Don C. Richter

9
Conspiring Noses

When my son was seven I took him on a fall camping trip in the north Georgia mountains. We pitched our tent on the banks of a lake aflame with the reflection of vivid red and yellow leaves. After a sound night's sleep we set out to hike the nearby Birdsong Trail. As we approached the trailhead, I noticed a huge log with a white cloth draped over it. We walked nearer and discovered it was a baby receiving blanket. But not just any blanket!

"Dad, that's Lydia's blankie," my son whispered, almost reverently.

"What?" I asked.

"That's Lydia's blankie. See, it has pink bunnies on it." Lydia was a five-year-old family friend from Atlanta. What my son said was plausible, since her family had camped at this same site the previous weekend. But I had my doubts.

"Jonathan, I just spoke with Fernando (Lydia's dad) the other day. We talked about their trip, and he didn't mention anything about Lydia losing her blankie. You know how important that blankie is to her. She never goes anywhere without it. She'd be devastated if she lost it. If she had lost it out here, it would have been a big deal. I'm sure Fernando would have said something about it. Besides, lots of blankies have pink bunnies on them."

"But Dad," my son persisted, now holding the blankie up to his face. "It smells like Lydia's blankie. It smells like her house. So it has to be her blankie!"

131

How could I argue with that? My son had spent a good bit of time at Lydia's house. And while his visual detective work might be disputable, this olfactory evidence seemed compelling. We tossed the blankie in our car and took it with us back to Atlanta. And before going home, we drove by Lydia's house. Her dad came out to greet us.

"How was your trip? Did you enjoy those beautiful leaves?"

"We sure did, Fernando. But we found something on the trail, and Jonathan is convinced it belongs to Lydia. Did she lose this on your camping trip?" I held out the blankie with pink bunnies.

"Oh my goodness!" Fernando exclaimed. "I can't believe it. Let me go get her." A few moments later, little Lydia came tearing out of the house. Her eyes got huge and round when she saw her lost-and-found blankie. Without saying a word, she grabbed it, ran inside, and stuck it in the freezer. That's what Lydia does when anybody else "hots" her blankie by holding it.

"Thank you so much, Jonathan, for bringing back Lydia's blankie," Fernando said. "She's been one sad girl all week long. Just this morning we were at Mass, and I asked her is she was getting used to 'substitute blankie'—that's what we call her blankie with blue bunnies. She said it was okay, but she still really missed her real blankie. So we prayed that God would help her find her missing blankie. And here you showed up with it!"

"Fernando, about what time was it when you and Lydia said that prayer?" I asked.

"Well, it was during Eucharist, so it was about 9:45."

"Amazing . . ." I smiled. "Because that's exactly when Jonathan and I found Lydia's blankie."

Potent Smells

Our noses can be a potent ally as we go out into the world. The nose can distinguish an estimated ten thousand different smells. Odor molecules are small and volatile, giving signals to our sense of smell over long distances. Think of how you can detect smoke from a distant fire even when you can't see or hear it. The flavor we "taste" is 80 to 90 percent aroma. We have an innate ability to detect bad, aversive smells. Even newborn babies make faces when exposed to offensive odors, such as rotten eggs. A baby recognizes its own mother's smell, and a mother recognizes her own baby's smell. Women, on the whole, have a more acute sense of smell than men.

It was no fluke that my son recognized Lydia's blankie most convincingly by using his nose. And it's no wonder that young children are so strongly attached to blankies that "smell like home." (Don't bleach that blankie!) A scent is a key to unlocking deep memory, as Marcel Proust demonstrated in *Remembrance of Things Past*. When Proust's character Marcel dips a madeleine (cookie) in lime-blossom tea, the grown-up man is immediately flooded with childhood memories of his Aunt Léonie, who used to serve madeleines every Sunday before Mass. Smells especially transport us back to childhood, whereas words and images shape more memories from the teen years through adulthood.

This striking connection between smell and memory is known as the "Proust effect." A familiar scent prompts whole memories, complete with associated emotions. The connection happens unconsciously and involuntarily. The olfactory nerves give smells privileged access to the limbic system, the "primitive brain" that orchestrates emotions. Ask any real estate agent how often odor is the decisive factor in a home sale. That's why agents advise sellers to bake cinnamon rolls when they're having an open house.

The perfume and scent industry is huge. In the U.S.A. alone, we spend more than $24 billion per year on scented products. North Americans pay dearly to control our odor environments! Once we have the means to "neutralize" odors, we lose our tolerance for smelly surroundings.

I caught my first whiff of this new nasal reality on a summer mission trip with teens shortly after the debut of the Stick Up deodorizer.

The tag line in the original ad campaign went something like, "This is a great place for a Stick Up." Teens delighted in quoting that line and did so emphatically whenever we boarded the van. I'll admit the van had a bit of locker-room bouquet, especially after a week of sweaty construction work. The odor was far from overwhelming in my estimation, but the teens thought otherwise. So by the time we headed for home, our van was equipped with no fewer than four deodorizers, volatizing every cubic centimeter of air we breathed. God forbid that one's body odor should offend one's travel companions!

Sacred Smells

The Stick Up incident was amusing and at the time seemed no more than a playful diversion. We never reflected on our group's olfactory obsession during our daily devotions. In hindsight I wish we had. We could have talked about the world of smells and pondered our aversion to natural body odors. Some people refuse to go on mission trips because they would feel embarrassed being unkempt around others for days on end. Even those who do go on trips make a dash for the shower after work to avoid offending others with their sweaty bodies.

I wish that I had talked with those teens about how scents sometimes separate people and sometimes bind them together. Noses accustomed to odor-neutral air can be overwhelmed when surrounded by strong smells, such as the pungent aroma of curry in Asian cooking. On the other hand, as church historian Martin Marty suggests, some religious communities are bound together by smells as much as by doctrine.

While in seminary I served in an Episcopal church that regularly held a "smells-and-bells service." That is, they dispersed incense and rang an altar bell during the consecration of the bread and wine. As a Presbyterian I was used to worship that filled my ears but not my nostrils. What a jolt to my system the first time the priest swung that smoking thurible in my direction! A cloud of aromatic haze enveloped me; it wafted through the sanctuary, giving the whole place a gauzy, mysterious atmosphere. I did not know but suspected that this was an ancient smell connecting me with the communion of saints down through the centuries.

I did not become an incense enthusiast during my internship with the Anglicans. Though I must admit, whenever I step into a church where the fragrance of incense lingers in the air, my body feels summoned to kneel at the altar rail and extend my hands. And on Epiphany, when I sing about three kings traveling afar to bring gifts to the Christ Child, my nose knows the peculiar smell of the frankincense they laid before him.

According to John's Gospel, Jesus is God's incarnate Son who lived fully in the world of smells. Jesus' first miracle was changing water into wine (John 2). We recall the stunned steward wondering why the best wine was saved until last. It was the wine's "nose," of course, that enabled the steward to sniff out the divine vintage. Before Jesus raises Lazarus, Martha makes it distinctly clear that he's dead: "Lord, already there is a stench because he has been dead four days" (John 11:39). No wonder Jesus shouted for that erstwhile mummy to come out of the tomb instead of going in there himself!

Soon enough Jesus would find his way into a tomb. On the heels of Lazarus's resuscitation, his sister Mary anoints Jesus' feet with costly perfume made of pure nard. The fragrance of this extravagant gift fills the entire house, John tells us. Jesus views her kindness as a last rite in preparation for his burial (John 12). In turn, Jesus washes his disciples' dusty, smelly feet (John 13). And who could miss the smell of those fish frying on the charcoal fire by the lakeshore, as the risen Lord prepares breakfast for his weary disciples (John 21)?

Conspiring in the Spirit

John recounts another appearance of the risen Lord in which the nose, if not the sense of smell, places a crucial role. When Jesus first appears to frightened disciples, he breathes on them and says,

"Receive the Holy Spirit. If you forgive the sins of any, they are forgiven them; if you retain the sins of any, they are retained" (John 20:22-23). Just as God breathed the breath of life into the first human (Gen. 2:7), God's Son now breathes new life into his band of followers. This new life has power to forgive sins and reconcile. As they inhale Jesus' own life-giving breath into their nostrils, disciples conspire—breathe together—in the Spirit. It is this holy conspiracy that sends the apostles forth with good courage from behind their locked doors and into all the world.

Paul, a latecomer as an apostle, speaks of "the fragrance that comes from knowing [Christ]" (2 Cor. 2:14). Paul claims that this fragrance, this saving knowledge, is being spread in every place through those who are following Christ. "For we are the aroma of Christ to God," Paul continues (2 Cor. 2:25). Even when things are not going well. Even when we feel inadequate to the task. God is gracious and works through our feeble efforts to accomplish great purposes. We carry the smell of salvation with us just as we carry the scent of our home in our clothing, often in spite of ourselves.

Gulf Coast Grace

In the spring of 2006 on the Gulf Coast of Mississippi, an early-morning knock at the front door startled an elderly couple awake. They found an energetic group of teenagers and adults huddled together on the remains of their front porch—hammers, paintbrushes, and cleaning supplies in hand.

"Good morning, ma'am, sir. We're a mission team from Long Beach Presbyterian Church. And we're here to clean and fix up your house today. May we come in?"

The frail man and woman glanced at each other, then behind them at the mess that had once been their proud home. Moldy Sheetrock, mud-caked furniture, rotten floorboards. The couple finally nodded and opened their door to this group of strangers, who quickly organized and set to work.

By the end of a long day, most of the fetid, flood-ravaged debris had been removed, and the house was well on its way toward recovery. The homeowners seemed overwhelmed with gratitude.

"You have no idea how much this means to us," the woman said through her tears. "We've been living like this for months, and not a soul has come by to check on us, to see whether we were still even alive."

"We had given up hope," the man agreed, with a quavering voice. "Just last night my wife and I decided that today would be our final day in this world. We had planned to end our lives tomorrow. . . . But then you showed up."

The mission volunteers absorbed this stunning confession. Then their leader gently pulled a set of papers from his back pocket. "Ma'am, we couldn't be the first contact you've had. We've got a work order for this house. Somebody had to come here before us to fill out this report."

The old man took the work order and studied it a few moments. Then he slowly shook his head. "You came to the wrong house. It's the right number but the wrong street. This house is several blocks over. I guess you couldn't tell with all the street signs missing."

In the providence of God, the "wrong" house turned out to be precisely the "right" house for the mission team to happen upon that day. How could these volunteers have known when they set out that morning that their service would have such immediate, profound effect? would toss a lifeline to an elderly couple drowning in despair?

We can never know for sure how our service in Christ's name will be received by others or make a discernable difference in the world. But we can be confident that God will bless our offering in ways beyond our imagining. And we trust that as we reach out to care for strangers near and far, we'll discover that we ourselves are already being cared for by

- a merciful God who never gives up on any of us, no matter how abandoned we may feel;

- a gracious God who shows up at our front door when we least expect it, when we had given up all hope;
- a redeeming God who cleans up the mess we've made, fills our lives with gospel fragrance, and returns us to the land of the living.

For the Journey

Think of a smell that unlocks a powerful memory for you. Ponder that memory and the emotions attached to it.

What products do you use around the home to sanitize, freshen, or neutralize your air? What smells like home to you?

What new odors or aromas have you noticed during your travels? What smell will you associate with this trip after returning home? Perhaps the smell of the van you spent hours riding in together?

Planning times to bathe is a vital logistical task for many mission-team leaders. Often hands-on service leaves team members dirty, sweaty, and eager for a shower. Teens already self-conscious about their appearance can get totally "freaked." It's one thing to look disheveled or to go without makeup. It's quite another thing to stink. How do we deal with body odors we're not used to confronting so directly?

What smells do you associate with holiness and mystery?

Bake bread in anticipation of sharing Communion together. While making the bread, discuss how the different ingredients in the bread are like different members of your faith community: some, like flour, provide the basic "stuff" of your common life; some, like oil and water, bind your community together; some, like salt, add flavor; others, like yeast, leaven the loaf. Continue your conversation near the kitchen oven so you can smell the aroma of the baking bread.

To conspire literally means "to breathe together." Songwriter Steve Kinzie plays on this meaning in his lyrics for "Breathe Together." Kinzie wrote this song two decades ago, during the U.S. arms race with the Soviet Union. The second stanza refers to the train carrying nuclear weapons to Trident submarines in the Pacific Northwest. How are Christians "conspiring in the spirit" these days? For what causes are we "breathing together"?

BREATHE TOGETHER

Lyrics and music © Steve Kinzie, 1986

We breathe together when we're dancing
We breathe together when we sing
I hope this world will always be around to breathe
Summer, fall, winter, and spring

Refrain
And we'll all breathe together
To break those chains of death
Conspiring in the spirit
'Til we all run out of breath

We breathe together to stop that train
We breathe together to help a refugee
We breathe together for a world
Where justice and peace are no conspiracy (*Refrain*)

We breathe together with the ones we love
Curled up through the night
We breathe together when we offer thanks
For another morning's light (*Refrain*)

We breathe together all around the world
With folks of every hue
Stranger, you can breathe along with me
Let me breathe along with you (*Refrain*)

Part III

Bless to me O God

My soul that comes from on high.

Bless to me O God

My body that is of earth.

Bless to me O God

Each thing my eye sees

Each sound my ear hears.

Bless to me O God

Each scent that goes to my nostrils

Each taste that goes to my lips

Each ray that guides my way.

—Phillip Newell

10
Building the Body for Mission

Building the body for mission begins at the Beginning. God spoke and breathed Creation, sending forth the Spirit to animate the waters and the earth. God's mission unfolded as Israel was called to receive God's blessing and be a blessing to all nations. God inspired prophets and sent them forth to proclaim God's judgment and justice, anger and mercy. At the "right time," God sent the Son into the world to redeem fallen creation. God's Spirit animated the church as a new creation, and the church was sent into the world to proclaim and participate in God's saving activity. You get the picture that our God is a sending God, not a static deity content to sit around all day on a throne. God is on the move. God is on a mission.

When any congregation today sends forth a mission team, that effort is not a random new fad or just a special project. The church universal from its conception was sent even as it was gathered. When Jesus' first disciples gathered to worship and enjoy like-minded fellowship (*koinonia*), they consulted the ancient equivalent of MapQuest to find the best route to Asia Minor. Disciples became known as apostles, the "sent ones."

In his parting words before ascending into heaven, Jesus commissions his band of followers into God's sending activity: "You will receive power when the Holy Spirit has come upon you; and you will be my witnesses in Jerusalem, in all Judea and Samaria, and to the ends of the earth" (Acts 1:8). Notice how Jesus avoids pitting "local mission" against "global mission." The apostles are to bear witness to the gospel right here at home (Jerusalem), throughout the region (Judea and Samaria), as well as internationally (to the ends of the earth). And that is indeed what happened and the reason the Christian movement spread so widely to become a major world religion.

Abundance, Not Scarcity

The local-versus-global mission argument is fueled by an underlying suspicion of scarcity. The argument goes like this: "We barely have enough resources to take care of our own and our immediate neighbors. We don't need to be going halfway around the world to serve when there's plenty of need in our own backyard." Ironically, Christians in North America, the land of abundance, voice this argument most often. African Christians embrace an ethic of abundance, even when natural resources seem scarce. Perhaps that's why Christianity is flourishing on the African continent, which now has the largest number of active, practicing Christians in the world.

An attitude of abundance grows out of trust that God is gracious and gives us everything we need to worship God and to be God's faithful companions. Throughout scripture, beginning in the bountiful garden of Eden, humanity has had to contend with a God who is too much, too extravagant, too prodigal. Jesus made tangible this God of abundance, summoning more fish than the nets could hold, breaking more bread than the crowd could eat, healing more often than the authorities allowed, forgiving more sins than anyone thought possible. Jesus invites us to join him in living abundant life. His invitation is startling good news for those who suspect that life mainly requires managing scarcity.

Today some Christian congregations are being transformed as they accept Jesus' invitation to live abundant lives. These congregations no longer hoard time, talents, and treasure for themselves. They actively promote a culture of mission among their members. In such a congregation, hands-on involvement in sponsoring and going on mission trips is not optional but becomes the heart of the community's self-understanding, the core of their corporate character.

Peachtree Presbyterian Church in Atlanta has intentionally developed a *culture of mission* during recent years. In addition to financial support for local and regional ministries, members are encouraged to join in hands-on outreach efforts. The church has long sponsored overseas missionaries, yet Peachtree now also employs a full-time director of global ministry and annually sends almost twenty mission teams to work with partner congregations around the globe. Through active service with those in need, Peachtree members create direct, personal ties with communities from Brazil to Malawi. These ongoing partnerships challenge this affluent congregation to share its abundance and its mission with neighbors near and far.

> *Creating a culture of mission doesn't just mean sending teams out. It also means receiving mission teams, providing hospitality as others engage in mission projects in our own backyards.*

Creating a culture of mission doesn't just mean sending teams out. It also means receiving mission teams, providing hospitality as others engage in mission projects in our own backyards.

Saint John's Lutheran Church in downtown Knoxville, Tennessee, sponsors a summer program in which out-of-town youth groups share the congregation's urban ministry. Saint John's equipped a building with showers and sleeping facilities and trained their youth to host visiting mission teams. To their delight, congregation members have discovered that creating a culture of mission has also created a culture of call among their members. Several young adults—who as teenagers learned to be welcoming hosts—are now on the road toward ordained ministry.

The Mutual Mission Youth Exchange is a partnership between the Presbytery of Saint Augustine, Florida, and Jamaica Ecumenical Mutual Mission (Moravian, Methodist, and Congregational churches in Jamaica). Each summer ten Presbyterian youth from northeast Florida serve in mission with ten youth from JEMM congregations. For one week, both groups join together for a mission project in Florida. For the second week, the entire group travels to Jamaica to serve in mission together there. Youth and adult participants experience mission as *mutual aid* that involves receiving as well as sending, hosting as well as being the guests.

How does your congregation counter fear of scarcity with Jesus' gospel of abundance? How are you cultivating a culture of mission? If I were a first-time visitor on a Sunday morning, would I be able to tell that your congregation has a passion for the global church? Does your Christian education program for all ages pay attention to the church beyond our national borders? Do bulletin boards and other visuals throughout the building communicate a concern for global mission? In the prayers, preaching, and music of worship liturgy, will I hear stories and songs of Christian communities from faraway lands? In every season, is your congregation preparing to send and receive mission teams? Consider three concrete ways to enhance the culture of mission within your ministry setting.

Count the Cost

The church goes forth confidently in mission, trusting in God's abundance every step of the way. Because we trust God to provide, we are open and transparent with regard to funding a mission trip. We don't resort to "hidden costs" or clandestine budget maneuvers to mask expenses. Congregations deserve to know the actual costs of sponsoring such ventures. They also need to reckon with what the same amount of money could support if donated to the group being served. Jo Ann Van Engen offers this example in her essay "The Cost of Short Term Missions":

A group of eighteen students raised $25,000 to fly to Honduras for spring break. They painted an orphanage, cleaned the playground, and played with the children. Everyone had a great time, and the children loved the extra attention. One student commented: "My trip to Honduras was such a blessing! It was amazing the way the staff cared for those children. I really grew as a Christian there."

The Honduran orphanage's yearly budget is $45,000. That covers the staff's salaries, building maintenance, and food and clothes for the children. One staff member there confided, "The amount that group raised for their week here is more than half our working budget. We could have done so much with that money."

Van Engen doesn't recount this conversation as a deal-breaker. She believes that short-term mission trips are justified when properly structured. She recommends that a group donate as much money to support the projects visited as it spends paying for the trip. This practice effectively doubles the cost of a trip and may seem beyond the reach of many congregations. At the very least Van Engen urges mission teams to tithe—give 10 percent of all funds raised toward direct support of their mission partners.

Are you communicating to your congregation the total cost of a mission trip? Or does the actual amount seem too extravagant and embarrassing? If this is first and foremost a mission of the *entire* congregation and not the whim of a subgroup, how can you bring the whole community on board in funding the initiative? Do numerous nickel-and-dime fund-raisers signal that the mission trip is a peripheral rather than a central activity of the church? Better to sponsor one big fund-raising event and rely on the church's outreach budget and participant contributions to underwrite remaining costs. Explain that a portion of your costs will be a direct donation to your mission partner.

Cultivate Partnerships

Mention of mission partners brings us to another way we build the body for faithful travel. In order to sustain the relationships and projects initiated by short-term mission teams, begin to cultivate long-term mission partnerships. While a congregation serves as an ideal mission partner, your faith community could also be called to a fruitful, ongoing partnership with a school, orphanage, or service agency. Discerning such a calling is a mutual—not unilateral—activity, because mission partners *serve together* in ministry, working and playing, rejoicing and grieving as members of one body, the body of Christ.

In 1993 the Presbytery of Western North Carolina entered into a mission partnership with two presbyteries in Guatemala. This relationship has been a constructive, ecclesial response to years of U.S. military and political intervention throughout Central America. Presbyterians from over one hundred congregations in Western North Carolina now serve in mutual mission with nearly thirty sister congregations in Guatemala. Delegations regularly travel in both directions, so that hosts become guests and guests become hosts. As you read these words, a congregation in one country is probably hosting neighbors from the other country.

In June 2002 my fifteen-year-old son, Jonathan, and I participated in the mission partnership between Grace Covenant Presbyterian (Asheville, NC) and the Jerusalem Presbyterian Church in Coatepeque. The Guatemalan congregation of thirty families—with only two automobiles—bent over backward to host our mission team of fourteen U.S. teens and adults. They welcomed us into their homes and into their lives. They were attentive to our every need, even before we asked. Together, we built concrete floor slabs and planted gardens, shared meals and prayers, sang and danced.

Our friendships and care for one another continued long after the Grace Covenant group returned home. When Jonathan had his first fender bender a year later, he received e-mail that very afternoon from a Jerusalem Church member. She had heard about his accident and wanted my son to know that their congregation would pray for him in evening worship. This embrace by brothers and sisters in Christ from far away enlarged Jonathan's view of the church beyond his local parish.

Likewise, one's home parish takes on greater depth and significance as the global church enriches the local by bestowing varieties of gifts, services, and activities (1 Cor. 12:4-11). Paul's description of the church as an *interdependent body* teaches us how mission partnerships can be mutual even in the face of glaring disparities. In what we might call ecclesial anatomy, members of the body are interrelated in such a way that each member requires the other members (1 Cor. 12:12-31). So while economic analysis takes note of the superior financial status of a U.S. congregation compared to a Guatemalan congregation, ecclesial anatomy names the needs and celebrates the gifts of both groups. Political analysis remarks on the power North Americans have over Central Americans; ecclesial anatomy looks for ways to share power across boundaries and borders.

While we need to acknowledge, confess, and remedy the reality of wealth and power disparities, these conditions don't tell the whole story. There's much more to see when we observe through the eyes of faith. Consider the experience of Henri Nouwen, who reflects on ministry with people in Central and South America in his journal *¡Gracias!* Nouwen echoes the apostle Paul when he writes:

> After many centuries of missionary work during which we, the people of the north, tried to give them, the people of the south, what we felt they needed, we have now come to realize that our very first vocation is to receive their gifts to us and say thanks. A treasure lies hidden in the soul of Latin America, a spiritual treasure to be recognized as a gift for us who live in the illusion of power and self-control. It is the treasure of gratitude that can help us to break through the walls of our individual and collective self-righteousness and can prevent us from destroying ourselves and our planet in the futile attempt to hold onto what we consider our own. If I have any vocation in Latin America, it is the vocation

to receive from the people the gifts they have to offer us and to bring these gifts back up north for our own conversion and healing.

Following in the footsteps of Nouwen, thousands of North American groups have been led to mission outreach in Mexico, Central and South America. We are called to serve, to receive gifts, to stand in solidarity with strangers who become brothers and sisters in Christ. As we pay attention to the lives of neighbors to the south, we advocate for foreign policy that will benefit rather than harm them in their struggle against poverty, hunger, and disease. And most importantly, we learn to say *gracias*.

If your congregation or faith community doesn't already have domestic and international mission partners, where in the world is God calling you to build such relationships? For reasons suggested above, I encourage North American groups to cultivate a partnership with a faith community south of the U.S. border. Here in this country, Gulf Coast communities will continue to need recovery efforts for the foreseeable future. Most regional church judicatories (synods, dioceses, conferences, presbyteries) encourage participation in their established partnerships. Start by exploring these existing networks.

Screen Agencies

Direct, long-term relationships with mission partners are optimal, but many mission teams rely on agencies and intermediaries to line up mission projects and arrange on-site logistics. Faithful mission travel requires a set of criteria for screening these agencies. Here are several basic questions to ask yourselves. Add concerns particular to your own faith community and situation.

- *Will the agency be a good steward of our money?* How will our money be spent, and what percentage does the agency keep for administration? (Tell the agency your congregation needs this information—transparency in counting the cost.)

- *Is the agency a good steward of the environment?* Mission projects that involve home repair may generate lots of trash. But being on the road is no reason for mission teams to abandon conservation practices. I attended a weeklong summer work camp in which four hundred teens and adults stayed in a high school while refurbishing fifty homes in a local community. No provisions were made for daily recycling of a mountain of plastic bottles and aluminum cans. Consider the implicit teaching: when we're serving others in the name of Jesus, environmental concerns don't really matter.

  When mission includes caring for the earth as well as for people, body building will include environmental stewardship opportunities. A mission team to Kenya spent several days planting trees. They were inspired by the story of Clarence Jordan, the founder of Koinonia, an intentional Christian community in Georgia. When on a cold, rainy day, Jordan was asked skeptically why he was planting pecan trees that would take twenty-five years to produce a cash crop, he replied, "I'm planting them for the people that are coming after me."

  Being faithful doesn't guarantee that we'll see the results of the work we've done within our lifetime. This is especially so when we work on behalf of the ecosystem. Being faithful means trusting that others will continue the work and that God will see it through.

- *Is the agency a stakeholder in the community being served?* Does the agency have an investment in this place and an ongoing relationship built on mutual trust? And has the agency been invited by the community to serve?

  David Knecht, a veteran youth leader in the Chicago area (Hinsdale), coordinates summer mission trips through Youth-Works. David finds that this agency cultivates a long-term, respectful relationship with every community being served. Because of their reputation and practices, YouthWorks has been welcomed onto many American Indian reservations where mutual trust is paramount. YouthWorks regional directors and on-site staff (mostly college students) are in place and well prepared before youth groups arrive.

- *Is the agency reliable?* In his years of experience with YouthWorks, David appreciates that they host and support his group as contracted. David advises, however, that mission teams must still negotiate expectations once they arrive on site. Even the most conscientious hosts cannot anticipate all contingencies. David realizes that "there's the trip you plan for, and then there's the trip you take." While on the road, he and his leadership team are prepared to devise a "Plan B" whenever necessary, which it often is.

- *Does the agency promote bridging and bonding for both groups?* Robert Putnam distinguishes between two forms of social capital: the capacity to bridge between different groups, and the capacity to bond within a distinct group. With respect to bridge building, find out whether planned activities will promote healthy partnership between the mission team and the community being served. With respect to bonding, you can request activities that strengthen relationships among mission-team members. Also consider how your outreach efforts will nurture relationships among those being served. For example, giving gifts to some but not all may stir up resentment after a team leaves. Ask yourself, *In what ways can our service among these people strengthen rather than weaken their communal bonds?*

- *Does the agency support a "safe sanctuary" policy for minors?* Many congregations now have a policy in place to protect young people and adults from potential sexual abuse. One basic provision is that when youth and adults serve in ministry together, there must always be more than two persons in the room (car, etc.) at a given time. Make sure that the mission site will honor your safe sanctuary policy, maintaining appropriate boundaries for whatever groups are present.

Simulate Challenges

Some people like to jump feetfirst into novel situations, but most of us prefer to build "scaffolding" beforehand so that we have something dependable to stand on. When my daughter discovered she would need a combination lock for her fourth-grade locker, for example, she was eager to buy the lock weeks in advance to practice dialing the right sequence of numbers. Practicing with the lock helped her gain confidence about one scary aspect of her school situation.

Simulation experiences can help participants anticipate some of the conditions they will encounter on their mission trip. A good simulation provides an approximation of an experience, a way of taking risks within a safe holding environment.

Calvin Center is a Presbyterian camp and conference center just south of Atlanta. The Center's Global Village seems a world away from suburban Atlanta; it's designed to simulate conditions in rural Haiti. Mission teams can spend a few hours or a few days in this setting, sleeping in cinder-block huts, drawing water from a well, foraging for firewood to cook simple meals, usually beans and rice. Health-risk factors such as malaria are not the same as in Haiti. But the Global Village gives guests a taste of what life is like in a Two-Thirds World context.

Heifer International also provides an array of learning centers in Arkansas, Massachusetts, California, and Michigan (Global Village). At Heifer Ranch in Perryville, Arkansas, students from nearby Hendrix College immerse themselves in Global Village 2, where they are randomly assigned to the daily lifestyle of different countries. A group assigned to the Guatemala House considered themselves fortunate to have access to water and to have meat available as a food item. The meat, however, was a rabbit; the group had to vote whether to kill and eat it. Anyone who wanted meat had to watch the butchering. As one student remarked, "It helps you realize that meat doesn't just come from the grocery store." No doubt this student will weigh her diet options differently after this "food with a face" encounter.

Plan Ways to Share Your Story

Mission teams often share their stories in Sunday worship after returning home. Some teams design and lead worship, featuring songs and prayers learned from mission partners. As a fund-raising event, one youth group sells "shares" in their mission trip. Following the trip, mission-team participants host a "shareholder meeting" to tell the story of their trip over a feast of donated desserts.

Strategize well in advance when and how your mission team will share its story with others, especially with your congregation. Assign several mission-team members the responsibility for photographing and documenting the entire trip. Then give team members an opportunity to rehearse telling their stories before returning home.

Plan to Reflect

Veteran mission-trip leader Larry Coulter builds in a full day of reflection for his group at the conclusion of every trip. The retreat day may be held while the group is still on the road after returning home at a nearby camp or conference center. Whenever it occurs, Larry intentionally creates time and space for participants to contemplate what they've experienced and ponder what God is calling them to do—as individuals and as a group—as they return to daily life with new awareness and deeper compassion.

Setting aside a full day for reflection can be a challenge because everyone wants to get back to home and family. But a retreat day can be pivotal in sustaining the power and significance of a mission trip. Focused conversation prompts mission-team members to tell travel stories shaped by biblical themes and theological questions. The group creates a reservoir of shared memory to respond to the inevitable question, "So, how was your trip?"

For Larry and his leadership team the mission-trip retreat marks the first day of an intentional six-month reflection process. They plan regular group gatherings and local mission projects to keep alive the gifts of compassion awakened during the trip.

Blessing

When God calls Abraham and Sarah to pack their bags and move to a new land, God promises to bless this elderly couple and to make them and their descendants a blessing to others (Gen. 12). They are not blessed because of how pious they are or because of how well they dress or because they run with the right crowd. God is simply in the business of blessing. And so it's not surprising that God lays hands upon two ordinary, undeserving people and sends them forth to flourish for the sake of the world.

When God sends us forth to serve in mission in our day and time, God lays hands on us and blesses us on our way. And like Abraham and Sarah, we too are called to be a blessing to others as we go. What does it mean to be blessed?

In the novel *Gilead*, an aging minister recalls a childhood memory of baptizing a litter of kittens—by sprinkling, not dunking! "Everyone has petted a cat," he observes, "but to touch one like that, with the pure intention of blessing it, is a very different thing." The minister, who has baptized many people throughout his career, goes on to say that "there's a reality in blessing. . . . It doesn't enhance sacredness, but it acknowledges it, and there is a power in that."

To be blessed is to have someone acknowledge your sacredness—as well as your vulnerability. Jesus, overruling his disciples' objections, takes little children in his arms, lays his hands on them, and blesses them (Mark 10:13-16). He touches the most vulnerable ones in our midst and by his blessing confirms their sacred worth. By blessing the children, Jesus reminds us that human dignity is ascribed rather than achieved. Mark's Gospel punctuates this lesson with Jesus' next encounter. A man who has achieved wealth and virtue is unwilling to sell his possessions, give the money away, and become a disciple (10:17-31). Jesus loves him and wants to bless the man just as he blessed the children—because of who the man is, not because of what he's accomplished. A blessing, like grace, is a gift to receive, not a reward to be earned. How hard it is to receive and give blessing when we assume it must be merited.

Whether we literally or figuratively lay hands on someone, the physical act of blessing engages the whole body. We bless with our eyes and with our touch and with our words. In a world that knows many ways to curse, we bless. We bless all creatures great and small. We bless our Creator. And we bless one another, honoring bodies that are as sacred as they are vulnerable. Wherever we serve in Jesus' name, we give and receive blessing. In this tangible, powerful way we participate in building up the body of Christ.

For the Journey

Read Jesus' commissioning words in Acts 1:8, substituting your mission team's location as illustrated:

"You will receive power when the Holy Spirit has come upon you; and you will be my witnesses in Decatur (*home*), in all Georgia (*state*) and the Southeast (*region*), and to the ends of the earth." Identify ways your congregation or group is fulfilling its commission by serving in each region.

Share a meal in which each person contributes a food item costing $2 or less. As you eat, read John's account of Jesus feeding of the five thousand (John 6:1-14). Tell stories about times when abundance emerged out of what appeared to be scarcity.

Read 1 Corinthians 12. How is the image of the many members of the body of Christ reflected in your mission team? In what ways might those with special needs—such as disabilities or health conditions— become "indispensable" to the body as you serve together in mission?

Plan a strategy for recycling while on the road, for making your mission trip green and eco-friendly. Option: present a daily "green award" to a team member who embodies environmental stewardship, even in small way.

Count the cost for your proposed trip. List several strategies for convincing the entire congregation to support and fund this outreach initiative. Decide how much will be donated to the group being served and how to make the case for including this expense in the trip budget.

If your mission team plans to enlist the aid of an agency or host group, list your criteria for evaluating and selecting that agency. List criteria in the form of questions you can ask during a phone interview.

If planning a youth-adult mission trip, review your "safe sanctuary" policy and discuss how this will apply while on the road.

Choose one skill that will be important for your mission team to have while on the road. Design a workshop to provide training in that skill. For example, a ropes course could teach team members how to work together to achieve a common goal. Or a food-preparation workshop could focus on specifics of safe food and water within the community your team will be serving.

Plan how to commission your mission team, especially within the context of a public worship gathering. Include a blessing ritual with laying on of hands.

Plan a capstone day for prayer, pondering, and processing at the conclusion of your trip. Identify key themes and guiding questions for
this day. Knowing these themes and questions in advance will help
you shape Bible study and reflection throughout the trip.

11
Resources for the Road

Listed in order of publication

Planning Guides and Workbooks

When God's People Travel Together: A Trip Leader's Planning Manual, by Debby Vial. Louisville, KY: Presbyterian Church (USA), 1999. A great resource for forms and checklists, especially useful in planning service travel.

Short-Term Missions Workbook: From Mission Tourists to Global Citizens, by Tim Dearborn. Downers Grove, IL: InterVarsity Press, 2003. Lesson plans for group orientation sessions prior to trip. Strong on cross-cultural awareness activities, personal reflection questions, and inventories.

Mission Trip Prep Kit: Complete Preparation for Your Students' Cross-Cultural Experience (Leader's Guide, Student Journal), by Kevin Johnson. Grand Rapids, MI: Youth Specialties, 2003. Leader's Guide includes step-by-step instructions for planning and debriefing a trip. Useful forms, checklists, and questions for leadership team to address. Student Journal includes personal devotionals and Bible studies for youth: three for before, six for during, and three for after the trip.

Welcome Forward: A Field Guide for Global Travelers, by Susan Lang and Rochelle Melander. Minneapolis: Division of Congregational Ministries (Evangelical Lutheran Church in America), 2005. This compact, accessible book includes sections that help prepare and plan for international trips, guides and tips for the journey, and reentry assistance. Sidebars offer leader tips, scriptural quotes, thought starters, and imagined "journal entries," each the source for further thought, discussion, or conversation. Supplemented by online resources (www.elca.org/globalmission/welcomeforward) and a companion music CD.

What About Short-Term Mission? by Julie Lupien. Longmont, CO: From Mission to Mission, 2006. A guide for participants and leaders of short-term mission experiences. Focuses on mining the meaning of the experience, and offers insightful questions and activities for the preparation phase, the insertion phase, and the return phase.

Theological Foundations for Mission

Missional Church: A Vision for the Sending of the Church in North America, edited by Darrell L. Guder. Grand Rapids, MI: William B. Eerdmans, 1998. Inspired by the concept *Missio Dei* (mission of God), the contributors to this book provide a biblical and theological mandate for mission, especially for the contemporary North American church.

Transforming Ventures: A Spiritual Guide for Volunteers in Mission, by Jane Ives. Nashville: Upper Room Books, 2000. Encourages participants to explore eight themes for spiritual growth before, during, and after their mission experience: discovering God at work; experiencing hospitality; making adjustments; liberating time; meeting Jesus; building a team; singing the Lord's song; and maturing in Christ.

A Mile in My Shoes: Cultivating Compassion, by Trevor Hudson. Nashville: Upper Room Books, 2005. Hudson, a wise spiritual director, describes dynamics of encounter, reflection, and transformation that are at the heart of a pilgrimage of compassion for groups and individuals.

Practicing Discernment with Youth: A Transformative Youth Ministry Approach, by David F. White. Cleveland, OH: Pilgrim Press, 2005. Great resource for engaging youth and adults in group reflection through Ignatian contemplative practices, consensus decision making, theater games, and silence.

Serving with Eyes Wide Open: Doing Short-Term Missions with Cultural Intelligence, by David Livermore. Ada, MI: Baker Books, 2006. Research-based study of mission within a global context. Livermore describes four ways to serve others with "cultural intelligence" (CQ): understand cross-cultural differences, interpret cues, persevere through cross-cultural conflict, and act appropriately.

Faithful Travel with Rick Steves at http://travelstore.ricksteves.com. This two-hour DVD features five programs for Christians who travel as tourists and pilgrims. Programs for mission team reflection include "Faithful Travel," "Weaving a Global Neighborhood," and "In the City for Good." All proceeds from this DVD go directly to Lutheran World Relief (www.lwr.org) to fight poverty worldwide.

Cloud of Witnesses: An Audio Journal on Youth, Church, and Culture, Volume 7: Mission at www.ptsem.edu/iym/cow/vol7/index.php. Online interviews include: Cultivating Compassion in Youth, Diary of a Mission Trip, Arts in Mission, and A Missional Church.

Books with Free PDF Leader Guides

Download at www.practicingourfaith.org:

Making Room: Recovering Hospitality as a Christian Tradition, by Christine D. Pohl. Grand Rapids, MI: William B. Eerdmans, 1999. Drawing on scripture, church history, and the experience of modern service communities, Pohl illustrates how communities and individuals can be blessed and transformed by greeting, welcoming, and sheltering others—especially strangers—in the name of Christ.

Receiving the Day: Christian Practices for Opening the Gift of Time, by Dorothy C. Bass. San Francisco: Jossey-Bass, 2001. For busy people who see time as an adversary to be managed, manipulated, and controlled, this book provides a fresh vision of time as a gift from God, waiting to be unwrapped and savored with true presence and delight.

Way to Live: Christian Practices for Teens, edited by Dorothy C. Bass and Don C. Richter. Nashville: Upper Room Books, 2002. Advocates a set of Christian practices that are crucial to human well-being and that, together, shape a life well lived. Reflecting on and growing stronger in such practices, teens encounter the possibility of a more faithful way of life, one that is both attuned to present-day needs and taught by ancient wisdom. See also www.waytolive.org.

Honoring the Body: Meditations on a Christian Practice, by Stephanie Paulsell. San Francisco: Jossey-Bass, 2003. Offers readers a guide for cherishing the human body as sacred and vulnerable; counters corrosive cultural messages that prevent us from knowing that we are children of God in our bodies as in our spirits.

Testimony: Talking Ourselves into Being Christian, by Thomas G. Long. San Francisco: Jossey-Bass, 2004. Explores how ordinary talking in our everyday lives—talking across the backyard fence, talk with our kids, talk about politics and the events of the day—can be sacred speech.

A Song to Sing, A Life to Live: Reflections on Music as Spiritual Practice, by Don Saliers and Emily Saliers. San Francisco: Jossey-Bass 2005. Church musician Don Saliers joins with daughter Emily Saliers of Indigo Girls fame to reflect on how music shapes our souls in relation to justice, grief, delight, healing, and hope.

Lord, Have Mercy: Praying for Justice with Conviction and Humility, by Claire E. Wolfteich. San Francisco: Jossey-Bass, 2006. A guide for those who want to move prayer beyond private devotion and engage faithfully with the questions, decisions, policies, and movements that shape our lives in society.

Just Eating? Practicing Our Faith at the Table, by Jennifer Halteman Schrock in collaboration with Advocate Health Care, Church World Service, and the Presbyterian Hunger Program. A seven-session curriculum for congregations that explores the relationship between the way we eat and the way we live. Order print copies through Presbyterian Distribution Service (800-524-2612), referencing the Participant Book (PDS #7436505361) or the Leader Guide (PDS #7436505362). Download free PDFs at www.practicingourfaith.org.

12
Prayers for the Journey

Grant, O Lord Jesus, that the ears which have heard the voice of your songs may be attuned to the sound of shalom; that the eyes which have seen your great love may also behold your blessed hope; that the tongues which have sung your praise may speak the truth in love; that the feet which have walked in your courts may walk in the region of light; and that the bodies which have received your living body may be restored in newness of life. (*Evangelical Lutheran Worship*, adapted)

—∿—

May the road rise up to meet you.
May the wind be always at your back.
May the sun shine warm upon your face;
the rains fall soft upon your fields,
and until we meet again,
may God hold you in the palm of God's hand.
(Traditional Irish blessing)

—∿—

Depart now in the fellowship of the Holy Spirit.
And as you go, remember:
in the goodness of God you were born into this world;
by the grace of God you have been kept all the day long,
even until this hour;
and by the love of God, fully revealed in the face of
Jesus, you are being redeemed. (John Claypool, adapted)

—◊◊◊—

God, who knit us together in a mother's womb,
help us honor what you have made.

Let us touch this masterpiece gently,
with reverence,
with delight,
blessing what you have blessed.

[worshipers touch body parts as they are blessed]

The face
For the housing of our thoughts
For the muscles of our emotion

The arms
For embracing what is sacred
For grasping, then releasing, your gifts.

The belly
For taking in nourishment
In some, for the nurture of new life.

The thighs
For carrying another's burden
For pushing off from the ground

The feet
For walking your paths of peace,
For standing on holy ground.

God, who formed these inward and outward parts
Fill us with wonder at such knowledge,
knowledge that we are wonderfully made. (Lani Wright)

—⟋⟍—

Lord Jesus Christ,
you invite the stranger and the sinner,
the outcast and the orphan into your wide embrace.
Like a nesting bird, you shelter and protect the weak
beneath your compassionate wings.
Hold us close and fill us with your love,
that we might welcome others as you first welcomed us.
(Susan Briehl, adapted)

—⟋⟍—

For God alone my soul waits in silence,
   for my hope is from [God].
[God] alone is my rock and my salvation,
   my fortress; I shall not be shaken.
On God rests my deliverance and my honor;
   my mighty rock, my refuge is in God.
Trust in [God] at all times, O people;
   pour out your heart before [God];
   God is a refuge for us. (Psalm 62:5-8, adapted)

O God, our rock and our refuge,
you give us every good gift.
Your love never lets us down.
Teach us to trust you more than power and possessions.
Free us from greed and fear so that, with all your people,
we might live securely in the wealth of your love,
poured out upon us in Jesus. (Susan Briehl)

—⚏—

God of nimble fingers,
at the flowering of creation
you took a mess of mud and shaped it
into your image:
male and female.

As we gather in your name, O loving Creator,
fashion us as your people.

Shape our feet of clay
into dance;
Shape our knees
into bending;
Shape our hands
into clasping;
Shape our water-logged lungs
into chorus;
Shape our chins
into upthrust resolve;
Shape our lips
into smile.
Shape us into your glad and faithful servants,
For the sake of your Son Jesus Christ, our Lord.
(Lani Wright, adapted)

—⚏—

In the beginning O God . . .
You formed my body
    and gave it breath.
Renew me this day
    in the image of your love,
O great God, grant me your light
O great God, grant me your grace
O great God, grant me

your joy this day
And let me be made pure
in the well of your health. (Philip Newell)

—∽—

O for a thousand tongues to sing
our great redeemer's name;
To sing beyond ourselves, extravagantly,
with abandonment,
beyond all our possibilities,
and all our fears,
and all our hopes...
to our redeemer dear, the antidote to our death,
the salve to our wounds,
the resolve of our destructiveness...
A thousand, a million, a trillion tongues,
more than our own,
more than our tradition,
more than our theology,
more than our understanding,
tongues around us,
tongues among us,
tongues from our silenced parts.
Tongues from us to you in freedom and in courage,
Finally ceding our lives and our loves to your good care.
Amen. (Walter Brueggemann)

—∽—

PRAYER OF SAINT PATRICK

Christ be with me,
Christ within me,
Christ behind me,
Christ before me,

Christ beside me,
Christ to win me,
Christ to comfort and restore me.

Christ beneath me,
Christ above me,
Christ in quiet,
Christ in danger,
Christ in hearts of all that love me,
Christ in mouth of friend and stranger.
(trans. by Cecil F. Alexander)

References

Introduction

The "good courage" prayer can be found in *Evangelical Lutheran Worship* (Minneapolis, MN: Augsburg Fortress, Publishers, 2006), 317. It comes from *Daily Prayer*, by Eric Milner-White and George Wallace Briggs (Oxford University Press). Christian Smith with Melinda Lundquist Denton report on the NSYR study in *Soul Searching: The Religious and Spiritual Lives of American Teenagers* (New York: Oxford University Press, 2005), 53–54. In *Congregation: Stories and Structures*, ed. Barbara G. Wheeler (Philadelphia: Fortress Press, 1987), James F. Hopewell describes a parish that on the same day celebrates Communion, fights over its music program, and fixes its plumbing. Hopewell states, "Mission for a congregation conceived in images that embrace the totality of parish experience has a different starting point than that which extracts from the whole a designated piety" (16). The theme "manna and mercy" is explored by Daniel Erlander in *Manna and Mercy* (Mercer Island,WA: The Order of Saints Martin and Teresa, 1992). The excerpt from Henri J.M. Nouwen's March 5 journal entry is from *¡Gracias! A Latin American Journal* (Maryknoll, NY: Orbis, 1983), 161–62.

PART I
Chapter 1: Why We Go

The opening prayer is from *Evangelical Lutheran Worship*, 86. The Brett Webb-Mitchell quotation is from *Follow Me: Christian Growth on the Pilgrim's Way* (New York: Church Publishing, 2006), 42. Jerome's homily on Psalm 95 (adapted for inclusive language) is quoted from *Pilgrimage: Past and Present in the World Religions*, by Simon Coleman and John Elsner

(Cambridge, MA: Harvard University Press, 1995), 81. I'm grateful to Carol Lytch for referring me to Gwen Kennedy Neville's sociocultural analysis of pilgrimage in *Kinship and Pilgrimage: Rituals of Reunion in American Protestant Culture* (New York: Oxford University Press, 2005). I transcribed comments by Rick Steves from his video program *Faithful Travel* (see Resources for the Road). The quotation by Katherine Turpin is from *Branded: Adolescents Converting from Consumer Faith* (Cleveland: Pilgrim Press, 2006), 102. Thomas Wolfe's novel *You Can't Go Home Again* was published posthumously in 1940 by Harper & Brothers (New York).

Chapter 2: Preparing to Lead

The opening prayer is attributed to fourth-century (CE) Saint Patrick of Ireland. Trevor Hudson describes "compassionate caring" in *A Mile in My Shoes* (Nashville: Upper Room Books, 2005), 24. Will Campbell recounts his civil rights experiences in *Brother to a Dragonfly* (New York: Seabury Press, 1977), 243–44. Quotations about adaptive leadership are from Ron Heifetz and Marty Linsky, *Leadership on the Line* (Boston: Harvard Business School Press, 2002) 2, 28, and 20. Scott Cormode's story of leader accountability is in *Making Spiritual Sense* (Nashville: Abingdon Press, 2006), 103. Stanley Hauerwas's sermon "Hating Mothers as the Way to Peace" is in *Exilic Preaching: Testimony for Christians in an Increasingly Hostile Culture*, edited by Erskine Clarke (Harrisburg, PA: Trinity International Press, 1998), 76–82.

PART II
Chapter 3: Attentive Eyes

The opening prayer is by Walter Brueggemann, from *Awed to Heaven, Rooted in Earth* (Minneapolis: Augsburg Fortress, 2003), 88. Joan Chittister tells the story of the Baja peninsula map in "Leading the Way: To Go Where There Is No Road and Leave a Path" (closing address at the 2001 National Catholic Educational Association convention) http://speakingoffaith.publicradio.org/programs/obedienceandaction/ch ittister-leadingtheway.shtml. Robert Frost's "Mending Wall" includes the lines "Something there is that doesn't love a wall, That wants it down." See *Robert Frost Poetry & Prose*, edited by Edward C. Lathem and Lawrance Thompson (New York: Holt, Rinehart, and Winston, 1972), 16–17. Emily's Thailand observations are from personal e-mail correspondence with Mary Emily Briehl Wells in February 2005. In *Vision and Character* (New York: Paulist Press, 1981), Craig Dykstra describes the interrelationship between the disciplines of repentance (letting go), prayer (paying attention), and service (compassionate presence). Mary Oliver's poem "Praying" is from *Thirst* (Boston: Beacon Press, 2006), 37. The rhythms of *ora et labora et lectio* are found in the Rule of Benedict, Chapter 48: http://www.osb.org/rb/text/rbemjo3.html#48. Some "For the Journey" ideas were adapted from *United Methodist Volunteers in Mission Training Manual for Mission Volunteers* (New York: General Board of Global Ministries, 2005). Nouwen's reflection about living with the poor is from *¡Gracias!* 160.

Chapter 4: Attuned Ears

The opening prayer is by Susan Briehl, *Way to Live Leader's Guide*, 118. Bonhoeffer's view of the Psalter as Jesus' songbook and prayer book is in *Life Together* from *Dietrich Bonhoeffer Works*, Vol. 5 (Minneapolis: Fortress Press, 1996), 54–55. I relate the Ethel Johnson story in the *Way to Live Leader's Guide*, 107. Susan Briehl's reflections on singing and her reference to Bruce Morrill's image of worship as "sounding bodies" are from personal correspondence in December 2006. Matt Weiler's Senegal story is from a January 2007 "Growing in Faith with Youth" course essay. "God, You Love the World" can be found at www.limestonepresbyterian .org/KenyaTripDevotional.htm

Chapter 5: Sturdy Backs

The opening prayer (adapted) by Lani Wright is from www.practicing ourfaith.org. The Barbara Kingsolver quotations are from *The Poisonwood Bible* (New York: HarperCollins, 1998), 246–47, 252.

Chapter 6: Beautiful Feet

I wrote the opening prayer for Eastertide 2007. For information about the Central Presbyterian Church Foot Clinic see www.central-presbyterian

.org/living_the_faith/foot_clinic.html. Grace Paulsen shared foot clinic reflections with me in January 2007 personal conversation. Stephanie Paulsell notes how foot washing reveals one's sacred vulnerability in *Honoring the Body* (San Francisco: Jossey-Bass, 2003), 29–34. Ryan Dunn recounts his mission-trip experience in a January 2007 "Growing in Faith with Youth" course essay. Accompaniment is the central theme for the ELCA vision of *Global Mission in the Twenty-first Century* (Chicago: Evangelical Lutheran Church in America); see www.elca.org /globalmission/policy/gm21full.pdf. The "catch and release" theme is developed by Richard A. Horsley and Neil Asher Silberman in *The Message and the Kingdom* (Minneapolis: Augsburg Fortress, 2002). Robert B. Kruschwitz describes the relationship between Judeans and Samaritans in "Wolves and Neighbors" for *Bound!* a mission-trip devotional guide. Thanks to Dan Erlander for insights about Saint Francis and the sultan. The legend of Saint Francis and the wolf is from www.amer-icancatholic.org/Features/Francis/stories.asp#wol.

Chapter 7: Open Hands

The opening prayer by Susan Briehl appears in *Way to Live Leader's Guide*, 56. The Truett Cathy quotation comes from www.truettcathy.com /about_recipe.asp

Chapter 8: Courageous Lips

The opening prayer by J. Bradley Wigger is from *Together We Pray* (Saint Louis: Chalice Press, 2005), 41. Statistics about Guatemala water contamination cited at www.livingwatersfortheworld.org/LWW_MO.php. Books that inform my understanding of the U.S. food economy include: Michael Pollan, *The Omnivore's Dilemma* (Penguin Press, 2006); *The Way We Eat: Why Our Food Choices Matter*, by Peter Singer and Jim Mason (Emmaus, PA: Rodale, 2006); *What To Eat*, by Marion Nestle (New York: North Point Press/Farrar, Strauss & Giroux, 2006); *Hungry Planet: What the World Eats*, by Peter Menzel and Faith D'Aluisio (Berkeley, CA: Ten Speed Press, 2005). "The modest water beheld its Lord, and blushed" is the translation of a Latin epigram by seventeenth-century British poet Richard Crashaw: *Nympha pudica Deum vidit, et erubuit* (in which Nympha symbolizes the water). John Shea retells Jesus' encounter with Zacchaeus in *Stories of Faith* (Chicago: Thomas More Press, 1980), 173–74. Gordon Lathrop describes early church table fellowship in *Holy People* (Philadelphia: Fortress, 1999), 188–97. David Hadley Jensen's description of eucharistic bread and cup are from "The Big Mac and The Lord's Table," *Insights*, Spring 2007, Vol. 122, No. 2, 5. Evagrius's view of gluttony is from *Spiritual Theology*, by Diogenes Allen (Cambridge, MA: Cowley Publications, 1997), 64–69. John Cassian's advice on fasting is described in the "Food" chapter of *Way to Live*, 73–74. Brian Wansink analyzes patterns of "mindless eating" in his book by that title (New York: Bantam, 2006). Marion Nestle's critique of supermarkets is from *What to Eat*, 17–24. Global water statistics cited by www.living waters-fortheworld.org

Chapter 9: Conspiring Noses

My opening prayer was inspired by my memories of smells of the four seasons. For research data on the sense of smell, see Tim Jacob's "Olfaction: A Tutorial on the Sense of Smell" (www.cf.ac.uk/biosi/staff/ jacob/teaching /sensory/olfact1.html#Memory) and Willander and Larsson's 2003 study of the "Proust effect" (www.cas.uio.no /Publications/Cas04no1/screen .pdf). Martin E. Marty's essay "Church Smells" appeared in *Christian Century*, March 8, 1995, Vol. 112, Issue 8, 279.

PART III
Chapter 10: Building the Body for Mission

The opening prayer by Phillip Newell is from *Celtic Prayers from Iona* (New York: Paulist Press, 1997), 40. I'm grateful to Presbyterian pastor Larry Coulter for insights regarding local, regional, and global mission. For information about the Mutual Mission Youth Exchange, see www.staugpres.org. Jo Ann Van Engen's essay "The Cost of Short-Term Mission Trips" was published by *The Other Side* (January/February 2000) and is now available at www.ajshonduras.org/joannsarticle.pdf. The Nouwen quotation is from *¡Gracias!* 188. The Clarence Jordan story is from www.koinonia partners.org/support/adopt-atree.html. Robert Putnam distinguishes between "bonding capital" and "bridging capital" in *Bowling Alone* (New

York: Simon & Schuster, 2000). "Heifer's Global Village Lets College Students Experience the Third World" is by Vicki Brown (www.gbhem .org/orientation/campusMinistries_article_pg1.asp?item_id=6). The cat baptism story comes from Marilynne Robinson, *Gilead* (New York: Farrar, Straus, & Giroux, 2004), 23.

Chapter 12: Prayers for the Journey

The prayers in this section are from the following sources, listed in order: *Evangelical Lutheran Worship*, 73; traditional Irish blessing; John Claypool's benediction, adapted, from www.crescenthillbaptistchurch.org/oldsite/bene dict.htm; Lani Wright, from practicing ourfaith.org; Susan Briehl, from *Way to Live Leader's Guide*, 92; Susan Briehl, from *Way to Live Leader's Guide*, 31; Lani Wright, from practicing ourfaith.org (adapted); Newell, *Celtic Prayers from Iona*, 25; Brueggemann, *Awed to Heaven, Rooted in Earth*, 9; Cecil F. Alexander's translation of "St. Patrick's Lorica."

—⁜—

About the Author

D ON C. RICHTER is associate director of the Valparaiso Project on the Education and Formation of People in Faith, Valparaiso University. With Dorothy C. Bass, he coedited *Way to Live: Christian Practices for Teens* (Upper Room Books, 2002). Don is a graduate of Davidson College (AB) and Princeton Theological Seminary (MDiv, PhD). An ordained minister in the Presbyterian Church (USA), Don has taught Christian education at Bethany Theological Seminary and at Candler School of Theology, where he was founding director of the Youth Theology Institute. Don currently lives in Decatur, Georgia, and is father of two children, Jonathan and Katherine.